LIFEBLOOD

How Successful Business Owners Achieve Wealth

by

Sam Frowine

Bloomington, IN Milton Keynes, UK

authorHOUSE

AuthorHouse™
1663 Liberty Drive, Suite 200
Bloomington, IN 47403
www.authorhouse.com
Phone: 1-800-839-8640

AuthorHouse™ UK Ltd.
500 Avebury Boulevard
Central Milton Keynes, MK9 2BE
www.authorhouse.co.uk
Phone: 08001974150

First published by AuthorHouse 6/16/2006

ISBN: 1-4259-2162-0 (sc)
ISBN: 1-4259-2163-9 (dj)

Library of Congress Control Number: 2006901864

Printed in the United States of America
Bloomington, Indiana

This book is printed on acid-free paper.

Dedication

**To my wife, Velda, and my Mom, Janet,
and to my children
Leslie, Sam, Molly and Andrew**

In loving memory to my Dad, Sam

Acknowledgements

This book would not exist if the owners in my life had not chosen to let me walk side by side with them on their journeys. They are the subject experts of this book; I am just the storyteller.

Paul Bennett is my business partner and friend for almost two decades. For half that time he has urged me to put my thoughts on business ownership and enterprise building in a book or in a journal so others could experience what we've experienced. Paul is the smartest strategist and deal guy I know and has intertwined his thoughts with mine so much that at times I am not sure which are my thoughts and which are his. He deserves much credit for shaping my thinking everyday on the realities of business ownership and the lifeblood of success.

Peg Robarchek is my other partner and writing soul mate. Peg is a journalist, fiction and real life writer, and a wise woman. Six years ago I asked Peg to help me edit and convert my piles of written works—hundreds, no, maybe thousands of pages—into publications digestible to the world. She accepted the challenge and since has been in my life almost every day, working away at the monumental task of editing my words and thoughts into valuable publications. She is an inspiration to me and has been a remarkable encourager when the demands of writing and the realities of keeping the business doors open seemed overwhelming.

Thanks to Robert Morris, editor with *American City Business Journals*, who saw the value of speaking to business owners through my column, *Business Wealth*. Thanks also to all the present and past employees of my companies. I am grateful for the extraordinary loyalty of so many who have chosen to help me build the enterprises that served as laboratories for testing the concepts and propositions of my work on business ownership. Especially, I want to thank Melinda Stanley, my assistant who selflessly works to ease the chaos and demands of my work life, helping me sort the urgent noise from the important stuff.

Anyone who hangs around me knows that my faith and vocational journeys are inextricably intertwined and that without the wisdom and encouragement of authentic leaders and the comfort of the Scriptures I would likely have folded my tent and headed back down Great Enterprise Mountain a long time ago. David Chadwick, an author, preacher and teacher inspired me to become a better student of God's word. Palmer Trice modeled for me the significance of relationship intimacy and encouragement as the bases for influencing others for good. Mike Moses challenges me to let God work his plan with the promise that he will do immeasurably more than I can hope or imagine. David, Palmer and Mike are a lineage of leaders within my faith community who have inspired me to pursue my calling with passion and courage.

Every business owner needs someone in their life who offers a steady voice that reminds them to never give up because their work is important and their purpose is significant. My wife, Velda, has been that to me for more than 21 years. She encourages me in my lonely hours and humbles me in my moments of euphoria. Thank you, Velda, for believing in me and giving me the conditions to pursue my dreams.
SEF

Owner Contributors

The following owners made a direct contribution to *Lifeblood,* either by taking time for an interview or allowing me to quote them or otherwise sharing their ownership journey with me. Countless other business owners who aren't listed here have made invaluable contributions over the years by elevating my insights and understanding of how business owners build wealth. My gratitude to all those listed here and to all those whose impact has been anonymous, behind the scenes or too deep to convey in words.
SEF

Rudy Alexander
The Elevator Channel

Francisco Alvarado
Alvacor, Inc.

Alan Barwick
Republic Electric

Mike Bartlett
American Coffee Company, Inc.

Buzz Bizzell
Bizzell & Partners

Ty Boyd
Pat Boyd
Ty Boyd Executive Learning Systems

Richard Brasser
Targeted Golf

Alex Bryant
East West Associates, Inc.

Slater Burroughs
Burroughs Safety Shoe Service

Bob Confoy
Mike Geraghty
Tim Condron
HomeGuard Inc.

J. Kevin Cobb
Max Smith
Grace Innovations, LLC

Donald Costner
Roger Costner
Brothers Air & Heat Inc.

George Couchell
Showmars Restaurants

Jeff Dudan
AdvantaClean

Stuart Fligel
Fligel's Uniform Company

Andrew Frowine
Cedar Works

Janet Frowine
Janet Frowine Antiques

Steven A. Frowine
Natural Wonders

Alex Fu
Tammy Fu
Shanghai Restaurant

Tad Geschickter
Jodi Geschickter
ST Motorsports

Mike Greene
Tana Greene
StrataForce

Dave Griffin
ProfIT/CS

Tom Grogan
Grogan Associates

Denny Hammack
Patterson Pope

John Hart
Jeff O'Keefe
Network Communications Technologies, Inc.

Gordon Henderson
Henderson Recreation Equipment Limited

Eric Hillman
Jeff Compton
Europa Sports

Linda Holden
The Linda Construction Company

Chuck Howard
Auto Bell Car Wash

Mike Hurd
Greg Phillips
Emporos Systems

Larry Hyatt
Hyatt Gun Shop
Hyatt Coin Shop

Paul Jamison
Corporate Creative

John Juba
Joni Juba
Juba Aluminum Products Company, Inc.

Dan Keenan
CIMTEC Automation LLC

Pete Lash
Beacon Partners

Eric Lerner
Action Plus Sportswear & Specialties

Dwayne Lewis
Ed Woolley
Paul Green
George Pinion
Flooring Solutions
Sub-Floor Solutions

Bill Lowry
Lowry, Haywood & Associates

Mark Maier
Omni Plastics

Jim McCabe
Racing Visions
and MiniFASTCAR

Mike Minter
Minter and Associates

Mike Moore
Educational Adventures

Dennis Moser
The Moser Group, Inc.

Mary Elizabeth Murphy
S.T.A.R. Resources

Charles Myers
Myers Park Mortgage

Julia Frowine Nestor
Jewels from Jul

Robert Norris
Wishart Norris Henninger & Pittman PA

Tim Parsons
Impact Financial Systems

Michael Peed Sr.
Woodworks, Inc.

David Pitts
Bill Gardner
Classic Graphics

Tony Pope
Chip Eleazer
Ecoscape Solutions Group

Dana Queen
Q-Trans Logistics

Dana Rader
Dana Rader Golf School

Barbara Frowine Ramsey
Mary Kay Cosmetics,
Independent Consultant

Scott Ramsey
Tic Toc Tire

Rob Rogers
Chick-fil-a

Ada Shapiro
Carolina Marketing Devices Inc.

Bob Shaw
Concentric Marketing

Dr. Morris Sheffer
EyeCare Clinic

Scott Spanbauer
BridgeBuilder

Todd Stancombe
Lewis Foreman
Enventys

Mike Stegall
Carolina Cool Carriers Inc.

Don Stremovihtg
Legacy Play Equipment, Inc.

Dalton Taylor
Artisan Shutters

Scott Toney
Camstar Systems, Inc.

Mary Tribble
Tribble Creative Group

Katie Tyler
Tyler 2 Construction

John Vieregg
Kelley Vieregg
Interiors Marketplace

Bill Walker
Media Evolved

Dick Washburn
Dorothy Washburn
Bob Washburn
Anne Washburn
The Chalet Club

Denny Watson
LogoNation, Inc.

Ed Weisiger Jr.
Carolina Tractor

Christian Werner
New World Mortgage

Randy White
TriCapital Financial Corporation

Scott Whittle
Richard Whittle
Southeast Equipment Service of
Charlotte, Inc.

Troy Wiseman
InvestLinc

Oscar Wong
Highland Brewing Company

Joan Zimmerman
Southern Shows

Author Biography

Working with business owners to achieve their goals is what drives Sam Frowine. For more than 20 years, he has been owner, CEO, managing partner or investor in more than a dozen enterprises—several very successful and a few not so successful. Sam is also the author of the ***Business Wealth*** column in ***The Charlotte Business Journal, Blueprint for Building Great Enterprise,*** and ***Foundations for Great Enterprise & True Wealth***; he is also creator of the Enterprise Builder System™ and the Summit retreat for launching business owners on their journey as Wealth Builders. He is founder and owner of The Performance Group, Performance Capital Group and the Institute for Business Owners, and Chairman of the Corporation for Great Enterprise. The focus of Sam's work is coaching business owners who are crossing the chasm that separates entrepreneurs from enterprise builders whose companies are the foundation for their portfolio wealth. Sam, whose roots are in Portsmouth, Ohio, holds a doctorate degree in developmental psychology from the University of Cincinnati, where he was a faculty member for seven years. He received his undergraduate and Master of Science degrees from Ohio State University. For more information, visit www.samfrowine.com.

Table of Contents

Wealth Builders Play
by
Smart Money Rules

I.   Learn to Earn: Business wealth is not measured by revenue; it is measured by what's left over at the end of the day.

II. Eyes on the Money: Never assume that anyone else will pay attention to the money. Only the owner has enough at stake to be constantly vigilant.

III. Make Cash Flow: Cash flow is the vehicle for turning the source of financial health—revenue—into the fruit of our financial health—profit.

IV. Avoid the Debt Sinkhole: When we gamble with debt, the stake is our freedom.

V.   Hedge Your Bets: Every failure traces back to a false assumption.

VI. Leverage Down: Under the surface of every business is untapped gold waiting to be mined.

VII. Think Like a Capitalist: Prepare for the day when an infusion of capital can elevate the wealth-building potential of the business.

INTRODUCTION

CRACKING THE BUSINESS WEALTH CODE

No one—*no one*—is in a better position to tap the wealth potential of the 21st Century economy than business owners.

It's been a long time in coming, but entrepreneurs are now recognized as the backbone of the U.S. economy. But recognition and respect are secondary to the fact that business owners now have the greatest potential for significant wealth simply because they are players in the number one game in town.

That's the good news.

Here's the bad news: Too many business owners will lose this opportunity—the very opportunity they've created for themselves and others—because they haven't learned the rules of the Business Wealth game.

You and I and the other 25 million-odd business owners in the U.S.[1] are leaders in the revolution that will re-invent and reinvigorate our economy and, along the way, provide us with unprecedented opportunities to build significant wealth.

In his books *The Millionaire Next Door* and *The Millionaire Mind*, Tom Stanley offers plenty of research to prove that self-employed people—entrepreneurs like us—are far more likely to be millionaires than those who work for others. Our dogged determination makes us winners. Stanley reports that 26% of the deca-millionaires (people with a net worth of $10 million or more) he studied were business owners; one in three of the millionaires were business owners. Others were retirees (many of whom had once been entrepreneurs), professionals,

CEOs of major corporations and those who inherited. In his first study, of the 80% of millionaires who were still working and not retired, more than two-thirds were business owners.

We're definitely in the right game.

But hold on. Don't get too heady. As with most euphoria, there's a dose of reality around the corner. This dose is sad: most of us will fall on the battlefield of the Entrepreneurial Revolution.

About 600,000 businesses fail every year. And every year, 600,000 optimistic entrepreneurs start new businesses.[2] Of the businesses that manage to keep their doors open, only about 4% will ever top $1 million in revenue. With every financial milestone--$5 million, $10 million, $20 million—the percentages drop.

I know the fears and I know the uncertainties. I'm a business owner—to be exact, I own four of them at the moment. My wife, Velda, says I'll own businesses until the day I die. I can't argue with that.

I've been a business owner for more than 20 years. I've been in manufacturing and I've been in service industries. Like every other business owner I know, I've sweated payroll, struggled to hold the line on overhead and stared at the ceiling in the middle of the night with revenue on my mind. I still do. Like a lot of business owners, I've bought and sold and turned around businesses. I've walked away from some of them with only the few dollars I needed to start over; others, I've sold for a return on my initial investment that ranged from adequate to satisfying to significant.

Inevitably, I start another business. I'm an entrepreneur; what else am I going to do?

When I started out, it was no badge of honor to be a business owner. I think it broke my mom's heart.

"Why can't you be like Joey?" she said when my old friend became an optometrist. "His mother's so proud."

In my first jobs I was a prison social worker, then a day care teacher. I earned a doctorate in developmental psychology and graduated to teaching University of Cincinnati students how to think. My mother was proud of me then. I wasn't exactly an optometrist, but at least I had "doctor" in front of my name.

But a university is no place for the entrepreneurial spirit.

I wanted to run my own show. Control my own destiny. And put some food on the table while I was at it—always a challenge on a professor's salary. Besides, I didn't like playing by anybody else's rules. I could always see a better way of doing things, but nobody in academia was interested.

So I thought up an idea for a business. I didn't get rich, but I did find a life-long passion for the art of business ownership.

Nobody's going to mistake me for the Donald Trump of small business, but I have walked the owner's walk for decades. I've been owner or investor of businesses in home building materials, manufacturing, printing, marketing and trade show exhibits. I've learned about distribution, production, human resource management. I've learned about business planning and forecasting.

I've also learned that none of those factors is the key to controlling my own destiny. The key is found in the art of business ownership as the vehicle for building wealth.

For the last dozen years, my consulting company has worked with the owners of closely held companies to optimize the wealth-building potential of their enterprises. We've built a model for achieving profitable and sustainable growth specifically tailored to the unique circumstances of private enterprise. So I work in the trenches every day with owners who are fighting to beat the odds. I've seen my share of business owners who are hanging on by a thread or churning money to keep the machine running or wrecking their lives on the brutal and unforgiving treadmill of business ownership.

I've also seen the owners who cross the chasm from start-up to sustainable, legacy-bound enterprise. They hit the $5 million mark or the $15 million mark. They expand or acquire or franchise. Some of them achieve financial independence. Those who cross that chasm seem to have found the formula for economic freedom. They belong to a different breed of owners.

Although I'm interested in all shapes and sizes of owners, I'm most interested in those who have found the key to building sustainable business wealth. Some call it freedom. I call them Wealth Builders. What do they know that the rest of us don't know?

For the last four years, I've been writing about the Wealth Builders' mindset, their decision-making process, their beliefs and values for *American City Business Journals*. I tell their stories and their stories reveal the roots of their successes—and the failures that have made them stronger. Their stories demonstrate the distinctive traits and characteristics that show up again and again in the men and women who have built significant wealth on the platform of private enterprise.

For more than a decade, I've been refining and integrating the best of these practices of highly successful business owners into a body of knowledge for business owners who desire to become Wealth Builders. This body of knowledge has become the Business Wealth Builder's Code; it separates the winners from the also-rans. The Code is based on the hard-earned wisdom of experience. My own, yes, but it's also drawn from all the business owners I've met over the years. Every one of them has contributed to the depth and breadth of the body of knowledge that makes up the Code.

The Wealth Builder's Code is not a simple how-to. It is not a step-by-step formula. It is a creed that anyone can adopt. It's less prescription than perspective shift. The Wealth Builder's Code affects the ways we orient to our role as business owners. It reveals a pathway for developing a powerful leadership model, a company culture that supports wealth-building principles, excellent execution against the strategies that lead to enterprise success and, ultimately, to greater economic success.

But most significantly, the Wealth Builder's Code shapes the business owner's beliefs and values about business ownership. It becomes a way to redefine ourselves as business owners who are elevating entrepreneurship to the status of leaders and innovators in the 21st Century economy.

My mother, by the way, walked through my business recently and gave it her blessing. Like the rest of the world in the 21st Century, she has come to esteem business owners and their significant role in our economy as never before.

The first critical component of the Wealth Builder's Code is adopting a new perspective and new practices around the resources of time and money. Time and money are the lifeblood resources of every business.

Lifeblood. Sounds heavy-duty. Exaggerated, maybe. Don't kid yourself. ***Lifeblood is the difference between the businesses that open their doors tomorrow and the ones who don't.*** Lifeblood is the difference between the mom-and-pops that never get ahead and the enterprises that have crossed the chasm and become economic machines.

Lifeblood is the business owner's lifeline.

Lifeblood is found in the relationship between time and money: Healthy and rhythmic cash flow buys time to refine the success formula of the business. Long-term, significant success occurs through mastering the game of protecting the lifeblood of the business. We do that by first recognizing that every decision, every choice, impacts the lifeblood of the business.

Sound pretty basic? A no-brainer?

Then why do the majority of business owners never master it?

This book focuses on what the Wealth Builder's Code tells us about the lifeblood resource of money.

Money: When we've got it, we've bought the time to survive another day. When we're out of it, we're out of time.

Money: It's the way we measure success and the way we measure failure.

Money: Most of us know more about how to get our hands on it than we know about how to keep it and grow it. Some of us know less about money than we know about anything else in our business.

But all of us, no matter what life stage our business is at, no matter what industry, no matter what our long-term objectives, can achieve greater success operating by the smart money rules that Wealth Builders use in their journey to economic freedom.

Welcome to the journey.

PART ONE

THE CHOICE TO BECOME A WEALTH BUILDER

THE WEALTH BUILDER'S CODE:

*Business owners who experience
long-term success have mastered
the game of protecting
the lifeblood of the business.*

Chapter One

Business Ownership: A Rich and Risky Game

"If we're not in it for the money, we won't be in it for long."

Business is risky. It's a high-stakes game and most of us lose our shirts. Everybody knows that.

Here's what **I** know: ***When you play by the rules, you can win the game.***

Wait a minute. We're business owners. We don't like rules. We won't play by the rules. We make up our own rules. Right?

All true. But 20-plus years in the world of business ownership have proven this to me: When we know the rules and calculate our choices based on those rules, we can win the game.

Some of us even win big—we build significant wealth on the platform of business ownership. In fact, according to Tom Stanley and William Danko in their book *The Millionaire Mind*, self-employed people are four times more likely to be millionaires than those who work for others.

Here's another statistic I like: at least 90% of new businesses **succeed**[3] if their founders are experienced entrepreneurs—ones who have figured out the rules and make decisions based on those rules.

Do you like those odds? *A 90% success rate.*

Hmm. Failure isn't a fact.

Of course, becoming a millionaire isn't a fact, either. The vast majority of business owners never achieve economic

Lifeblood Plus

In the last five years, the U.S. has seen:[i]

- Approximately 2.8 million start-ups
- Approximately 2.8 million closings
- Average business bankruptcies per year—36,000
- 33% of new employer businesses don't survive the first two years
- 56% go under within four years

freedom. Business ownership can also be the fast track to financial ruin. Numbers from the Small Business Administration's Office of Advocacy make it clear that even though failure isn't inevitable, it's certainly a probability.

In other words, the opportunity of business ownership comes with equal danger.

We all know statistics can be manipulated to prove just about anything. But my read on the statistics surrounding business ownership in today's economy goes like this:

- If you own your own business, your odds of creating wealth go up.
- If you have previous ownership experience, your odds of success go up.
- Therefore, if you've owned a business before, your odds of building enterprise wealth in subsequent businesses go up.

Isn't the next obvious question, "What do the successful owners know that I don't know?"

What's their edge? How do we increase our odds of being one of the ones who keep the doors open and one of the ones who make millions?

In my work, I help business owners answer that question every day. Time after time, I see how they lose and how they win. And the ones who win are the ones who learn to play by the rules that protect the lifeblood of their businesses.

How's your lifeblood? Robust? Or anemic?

SURPRISE! YOU'RE ANEMIC

How do you measure the health of your business? Do you look at revenue? Sales trends? The number of customers, both new and retained? Profit margin?

When all those numbers look pretty good, do you still find yourself shaking your head and asking, "What happened to all the money?"

Sales are good. Revenue is up. Customers are happy. So *why* are we struggling to make payroll? How did we get to be profit rich and cash poor?

Where'd the money go?

In many cases, the money went out the back door while we were paying attention to all the wrong metrics. Our eyes are on what's coming in, and if that looks good we relax. Then it's time to pay taxes or rent or payroll.

Where'd the money go?

Owners Speak:

"Founding another business before I started this one and having the ulcers early on helped. You know what to expect and what you can handle. The stomach aches are a little easier than the first time. New owners have no idea the gut pains you go through."

Bob Confoy
HomeGuard Inc.
Founded 2003

Making money is hard; hanging onto it is even harder. Dozens of variables determine the health of our cash flow and we try to keep them all in our heads as they morph, sometimes daily. As owners, every decision we make about the resources of our businesses ultimately impacts our cash flow, the lifeblood of our business.

We can have ample lines of credit. We can have impressive machinery or a world-class facility. We can even appear to be making money on the balance sheet. Yet we can still wake up one morning and discover that the lifeblood of our business has slowed to a trickle and we're headed for life support.

Where'd the money go?

YOUR CHOICE

Business ownership can be the source of tremendous wealth. It can also be the source of financial ruin. Opportunity versus danger. Which will it be for you?

The choice is yours. Not the bank's choice. Not even the marketplace or the consumer make the choice. It's *your* choice. And every choice you make can impact the lifeblood of the business.

Maybe your choices look like Donnie's.[1] Before he turned 30, he was making it, spending it, hiding it. Boat, plane, beautiful wife, the kind of house he couldn't have imagined when he was growing up watching his dad walk the treadmill everyday to make somebody else rich.

Those days were long gone; Donnie was the self-made man that American dreams are made of.

He'd started out laboring for somebody else, showing up at daybreak, leaving at sundown tired and dirty. He watched the owner—who barked out orders and kept his hands clean—hang onto the lion's share of the money while laborers like Donnie barely made enough to keep gas in the pickup truck.

Donnie decided he was going to be the boss.

He left that job and struck out on his own. Some people might have said he didn't have what it takes to succeed. He had no formal education, no leadership training, no bookkeeping skills. But Donnie was a hard worker, and dependable, traits he'd learned from his father.

---

[1] To protect the privacy of business owners, most names and other identifiers have been altered, except when the owner's full name is used.

People hired him, recommended him to others and hired him again. Soon Donnie had a couple of guys working for him. He worked at their side, earning their loyalty with his sweat and fair treatment.

Within ten years, Donnie employed more than a hundred people. His company was well-known in the industry, recognized in the community for its skyrocket growth. Donnie didn't have to get dirty any more. From the outside, he looked like a fat cat.

On the inside, he wasn't as happy as he'd been when he was scraping by, dreaming of the future. The leaders of his business didn't trust him. His plane was starting to bore him and the shine was off last year's luxury car. But he was getting rich. Wasn't he?

The banks didn't think so.

"You're close to bankruptcy," they told him when he needed an infusion of cash to tide him over a cash crunch.

Donnie's lifestyle choices had buried him and his business in debt. And debt was drying up the lifeblood of his business. Donnie thought the game was about getting his hands on plenty of money. But he didn't understand the real game; he wasn't playing by the right rules and he was about to lose it all.

Owners Speak

"In my first business I learned how much I don't know. That's certainly enabled me to open my eyes and ears in other businesses I've been part of. It's so imperative to have perseverance, focus, to face brutal facts."

Rudy Alexander
The Elevator Channel
Founded 2001; 18 employees.

Then there was Teri.

Teri was making choices, too. The same choices she swore she'd never make when her dad worked himself into an early grave trying to make a go of the family business. Teri stayed out of the business she blamed for taking her dad's life. Instead, she started her own company. *Her* business would be different.

As she approached 45, Teri looked in the mirror one morning and realized she was looking at her dad. She was working and deferring and working and hoarding and working and stressing. The money was piling up, but she was bankrupting her family emotionally and choking the life out of her business. She had a terrific nanny, but she was never home to see her kids off to school. Her husband was eyeing the door and wondering if he should tell the divorce attorney that his wife was having an affair with her company. And the business was strangling because Teri had dammed up the lifeblood of the business. She thought banking the money made her less vulnerable, so she didn't re-invest in the business. She didn't build infrastructure. She didn't build a team of leaders. She built a gerbil wheel she couldn't escape from.

Lifeblood Plus
Defining Money Choices

Business owners face choices that impact the lifeblood of the business every day. An owner's choices in four key areas may reveal telltale signs that he doesn't understand the game:

Ownership reward: Will ownership fund a lifestyle either by unreasonably high compensation or by charging off as "business expenses" such high-priced toys as cars, boats, beach houses, thus sending the message to the organization that it's okay to squander resources?

Compensation model: Will the business reward based on performance, establishing a modest pay base for employees with incentives for achieving clearly-defined objectives? Or will the business create an entitlement mentality with 1) higher base compensation; 2) the expectation of holiday bonuses and annual raises regardless of the financial state of the company; 3) failure to instill in company leaders a sense of ownership for financial results.

Internal profit centers: Will each department or division be held accountable for financial success by tracking revenue and expenses directly related to that department? Or will all revenue go into one big pot, making it difficult if not impossible to determine where the revenue is coming from and where profit leaks may be hiding?

Capital planning: Will ownership view the business as an asset to be invested in? Will ownership plan for the day when outside capital may be required, either through loans or outside investors?

Teri expected the chest pains to start any day. Her choices were killing her, destroying the business and wrecking her family.

People like Donnie and Teri are born with the entrepreneur gene. They seem to know instinctively what it's going to take to succeed. By all measures, they have everything they need for success. One is making tons of money but faces bankruptcy; the other is making tons of money and little by little destroying her life. Each of them makes a classic mistake with their money. They aren't playing smart with the lifeblood of their businesses. Donnie squanders his on expensive toys. Teri hoards hers instead of putting it to work improving the business.

They don't know what game they're playing. They think the game is about bringing in a lot of money; if they can do that, their thought process goes, everything else will take care of itself.

They don't understand that the game is about playing smart with the lifeblood of their businesses.

STRIKING IT RICH

Business ownership can be a gold mine. And entrepreneurs are born optimists. Despite those hard-luck statistics that show new businesses overwhelmingly fail, just hand us a pick-ax and we'll go for the gold. Remember, the SBA's Office of Advocacy estimates there were approximately 24.7 million small businesses in the U.S. in 2004. (Their definition of a small business is one with fewer than 500 employees.)

No wonder the numbers are so high. We're in an era when the status of business ownership has been elevated; we're seen as the vanguard, the standard-bearers of the U.S. economy, no longer the guys who couldn't hang onto a job in corporate America. As global outsourcing stirs up fears of economic instability, Americans wonder what's going to save them and the answer is clear: the entrepreneurial spirit that has always been the foundation of the American dream.

A 2005 New York Times story by Elizabeth Olson stated, "With corporate greed and boardroom scandals long in the headlines, entrepreneurs are swiftly replacing corporate titans as America's business idols."

Corporate America is out, entrepreneurship is in. A survey by Harris International, commissioned by Yahoo Small Business in 2005, found that one-third of American adults would like to start their own business within the next five years. So at a time when the number of business owners is soaring, there are millions more preparing to hang out their shingles in cyberspace or finding the courage to rent the storefront office on Main Street and follow a dream.

There's the opportunity: As owners of small enterprises, we're staking everything we own or hope to own for the chance to strike it rich.

And there's the danger: Most of us won't strike it rich; we'll lose the gamble because we don't know the rules. We're not even playing the right game.

Who's going to survive? You? Me? The guy around the corner who's outfitting his home office and praying he's got what it takes?

Many of us who find the right vein to mine will ultimately end up no better off than the guy who only came up with dust. For every business owner who captures the wealth, there are ten who squander it—because they haven't mastered the rules for protecting cash and its flow as if it were the lifeblood of their businesses.

We can love revenue and we can love profit, but never forget that profitable and consistent cash flow is the lifeblood of the business. It is the one measure that ultimately matters because without it you cannot survive.

Lifeblood Plus
The Numbers[ii]

According to the Small Business Administration, small businesses:

- Represent 99.7% of all employer firms;

- Employ half of all private sector employees;

- Pay 45% of total U.S. private payroll;

- Create more than 50% of non-farm private gross domestic product.

Show me the money

If we're not in it for the money, we won't be in it for long.

I don't know about you, but I'm obsessed with money. I don't know a business owner who isn't.

We wake up thinking about money. We measure every opportunity on how much revenue it will generate. We squawk about every dollar spent in our organizations. We don't count sheep in our sleep, we count receivables.

Even if money isn't our number one motivator, we all reach a point in the life of our businesses when money is the first thing on our minds when we wake up and the last thought drifting through our brains when we fall asleep at night.

Statistics seem to support the idea that money is precisely what business owners **should** obsess about.

When we've got money, we're successful. When we don't have money, we're a failure.

Remember those statistics indicating that a lot of people run out of money? If we trust Uncle Sam's numbers, almost 600,000 businesses fail every year.[4] What's responsible for that number? A Dun & Bradstreet report from some years ago listed 14 common causes for business failure;[5] the most common causes could be traced back to money. They centered around pricing, lack of capital, debt, lifestyle expenses and lack of knowledge about financial record-keeping and decision-making. Even causes not directly linked to money certainly link indirectly: lack of planning and no knowledge of suppliers.

Translation: these business owners made mistakes around money. They didn't make enough. They spent too much. They spent it on the wrong things or at the wrong time. The lifeblood of the businesses dried up, for any of a number of reasons that all come down to money.

Sooner or later, no matter what our original motives or dreams, the reality of business ownership is this: *If we're not in it for the money, we won't be in it for long.*

So for all of our obsessing about money, we're still making a lot of bad choices. I see it every day in my work with businesses owners. My own business supports business owners who want to cross the chasm that separates the great idea from the great enterprise. So we give them the tools to build infrastructure and organizational structure and leadership capabilities. We help them develop strategy and we untangle problems. We sell businesses. We find investment capital. Oh, and another minor matter—we help companies implement disciplined financial reporting.

Owners Speak:

"I didn't know how hard it was going to be. It's more stressful than people realize. Most people have an idea that they're going to go into business and draw a reasonable salary, but it's very seldom that's going to happen. The key is not being the smartest guy on the block, but being persistent. Most people quit and if they stayed with it and saw it through, more businesses would make it. But most people are scared. And rightly so."

Alan Barwick
Republic Electric
55 employees

Personally, I like to think business owners come through our door because they want to contribute to the happiness factor for their employees. Or because they want to maximize every part of their lives—physical, emotional, intellectual, spiritual. Maybe, I tell myself, they want to become better stewards of the resources they've been blessed with. In my ideal world, I want to believe that business owners are drawn to my company because they want to become the best business people or spouses or parents or community leaders they can be. Surely business owners who want the secrets of success have noble motives. Don't they?

Nah.

What drives business owners through my door? Money. They don't have enough of it. The Overhead Monster gobbles it up. The business leaks it. Their leaders demand more of it. They've figured out how to make a lot of it, but the effort to keep it up is killing them.

Inevitably, they've made wrong choices about the use of the lifeblood of their companies.

WHAT'S YOUR CHOICE?

Draining the lifeblood of a business starts with a choice that seems pretty straightforward, maybe even pretty harmless. The choice is often unconscious. The difference between owners who build wealth and those who struggle is frequently determined by their answer to one question: Will I use this business to foster a certain lifestyle today, or will I use it to build true wealth for the future?

What about you? Whether you know it or not, you've answered that question. Do you even know your answer, and the consequences it implies?

Our answer to that question places us in one of two camps. We are either the Lifestyle Owner or the Business Wealth Builder.

Which are you? And how does that affect your future, the legacy value of your business, and the future of the people you love?

Ownership Perspective

- Why did you decide to become a business owner?

- Do you keep a record or journal about the lessons, questions or insights derived along your journey as a business owner?

- When you read the statistics on business ownership, do they inspire, humble, threaten you, or all of the above?

THE WEALTH BUILDER'S CODE

*Business is a living organism;
the lifeblood that sustains it
must be protected.*

Chapter Two

Playing the Wealth Builder's Game

*"Most of us don't realize we've been playing blind
until we begin to smell failure."*

Business owners are a different breed.

We want to control our own destiny. We don't want anyone telling us what to do. Never tell us we can't, because we'll always find a way. And we won't play by anybody's rules.

We're cowboys.

And that's okay. The United States was built by pioneers and adventurers. Wondering what's over the next hill and how to get there is in our blood. Our land was settled, in large part, by men and women with the courage to cross an ocean that extended farther than the horizon. Our very form of government was conceived by visionaries who inspired a ragtag bunch of farmers to take on one of the greatest military powers in the world. Our nation spread from one sea to the other because of men and women who wanted the freedom offered by open spaces and ungoverned territories. Driven by an inventive spirit, these pioneers transformed into entrepreneurs who figured out how to do things others believed could not be done, or things no one else ever dreamed of. We flew. We rode in horseless carriages. We made the remarkable and the impossible commonplace—telephones and televisions and computers and space travel.

That same spirit of adventure flows through our veins today. It's a spirit that never goes away. We're entrepreneurs, waiting to unleash our energy and imagination at the right time. Times like these.

BUSINESS OWNER AS PIONEER

What will we build with our pioneering nature?

The entrepreneurial mindset has long been a cornerstone in the foundation of our country. If ours is indeed the land of opportunity, most of that opportunity came by way of far-sighted men and women who could envision how an acre of cotton could give birth to a factory for spinning thread or how a burger joint that operated like a factory could revolutionize the way America eats. Our discontent with the status quo and our dogged determination make us winners.

What territory has this uniquely American adventurer set out to conquer in the 21st Century?

The economy.

Entrepreneurs are the 21st Century pioneers who will redefine our economy. We are leaders in the Entrepreneurial Revolution that will secure our own future and the financial future of our society, as well. That's my prediction.

During the past 30 years, a new generation of revolutionaries has begun to determine the economic and social direction of our world. *This entrepreneurial revolution will exercise the single most powerful impact on how we live, work, learn and lead in this century and beyond.*

REVOLUTIONARY TIMES

By virtually any measure you can take, business ownership is the predominant economic trend of the 21st Century. And as global outsourcing dominates the thinking of Corporate America, the role of private enterprise in creating jobs becomes even more critical to our nation's economic health. The entrepreneurial revolution, led by pioneers and cowboys like us, has the power to boost our country's economic health by growing its wealth. It's happened before, early in the last century. Enterprising Americans set the stage for an unprecedented economic and technological boom that shaped the world of the 20th Century.

Lifeblood Plus
Revolutionary Numbers

Here's my prediction: Entrepreneurs are the 21st Century pioneers who will redefine our economy.

Those are bold words. The facts behind them are even bolder.

- In 2004, 19% of Americans between the ages of 18 and 54 were planning to start a new business—the highest percentage in the world

- More than 99% of all employers are small businesses

- Small businesses pay 45% of all private sector employees

- Small businesses generated 60-80% of net new jobs annually over the last decade

- Small firms generate 52% of all sales in the U.S. economy

- Small companies make up 96% of exporters of U.S. goods

- Minority-owned businesses in the U.S. increased by 168% during a 10-year period

- Of the 23 million firms in 2002, 6.9 percent were owned by Hispanic Americans, 5.2 percent by African Americans and 4.8 percent by Asian Americans

- Women own 34% of all businesses (approximately 8.5 million)—an 89% increase in the last decade

I was reminded of that in 1993, when I had just sold a successful business venture. I'd owned the company for eight years; a few smart moves had allowed me to realize a life-freeing profit.

I wasn't ready to retire, but I wasn't sure how to best steward the resources I'd just deposited in the bank. I had an idea I wanted to pursue, but I wanted to be sure it was the right place to invest my time and money.

To reach the right decision, I went to a solitary mountaintop retreat at Lake Lure, North Carolina, to spend some time in reflection and self-evaluation. In the library at the Chalet Club, where I stayed, an autographed book lying on a table caught my eye.

Lifeblood Plus

A Great Enterprise is a financially healthy business committed to continuous improvement and guided by values and principles, led by an owner with a sense of purpose, perpetuity and legacy.

Among Friends by James Newton was about the author's friendships with a singular group of brilliant and enterprising thinkers and doers who ignited great change during a time of deep societal and economic upheaval. Thomas Edison, Henry Ford, Harvey Firestone, Charles Lindbergh, and a scientist and surgeon named Alexis Carrel are synonymous with the legacy of leadership and innovation that brought the U.S. to economic and political prominence in the twentieth century.

I was struck, as I read the book, by the parallels between their time and ours. The first half of the 20th Century was a time of dramatic change. Our nation was in the midst of a classic paradigm shift that would revolutionize the way people lived. The simple act of putting people in automobiles changed their sense of time and space as profoundly as ours changed when we discovered that a click of the computer mouse could connect us to people and information around the world. The automobile, of course, was only one of the astounding changes—there were radio, motion pictures, telephone, flight, television.

Undergirded by the explosion in technology, these influential people had made immeasurable contributions to our nation's economy in the 20th Century.

This moment in time offers the same opportunity for entrepreneurs to write the story of the 21st Century and leave behind the legacy of another, equally profound economic revolution.

THE LIFESTYLER VS. THE WEALTH BUILDER

Are you part of the entrepreneurial revolution? Or are you a one-gun slinger content to conquer your own corner of the economic territory? The mindset of business owners falls into two distinct categories that define thoughts and behaviors around money, purpose and vision for the enterprise. Take a look at those divergent mindsets and how they impact the health and long-term viability of a business.

One is the Lifestyler. The other is the Business Wealth Builder.

First, meet the Lifestylers. Lifestylers' fundamental beliefs about their business is that it belongs to them and it is there to serve their needs. It is a vehicle for getting more of what they want in life. As typical entrepreneurs, that might mean more freedom—more time to spend with family or traveling or boating or reading. Some entrepreneurs want nothing more than a place to ply their trade—to keep it small so they can pour their energy into delivering on their special talents without the headaches that come with building an enterprise. That, too, can become a Lifestyle choice, if that desire becomes the litmus test for financial or growth decisions. For others, the desire is for more material rewards and the perks that come with projecting the image of power and affluence.

There is nothing wrong with those motives, as long as owners understand that these choices come with trade-offs.

Choosing the pursuit of more freedom, more time or more self-expression typically reflects the goals of the Quality-of-Lifestyler. The kind of life these owners want to live is more important to them than money, even significant money. A Quality-of-Lifestyler wants to keep it simple.

In today's uncertain world, that's an understandable priority. Instead of growing an enterprise, this breed of Lifestyler is satisfied with a simple entrepreneurial pursuit. These owners will have few, if any, employees. Maybe a home office. If the business has three or five or ten employees, everything still centers around ownership because of the owners' number one priority of maintaining quality of life.

Such a small business almost always becomes solely dependent on the owner. Earning potential hits a ceiling. The market value of the company is compromised because no one will buy or invest in a company that relies on one person to run the money machine.

Another type of Lifestyler chooses material comfort. Initially, that may look and feel like a quality of life choice. But there's a further pitfall that's hard to sidestep when material things become the goal. Image Lifestylers are born when the pursuit of possessions begins to drive

Lifeblood Plus
The Professionals' Lifestyle

Professionals—doctors and attorneys—with their own private practice may be Wealth Builders or Lifestylers. But in either case their circumstances aren't quite like the solo business owner or the entrepreneur who has decided to build an enterprise.

A professional practice typically generates significant income, unlike other solo owners. By society's definitions, most professionals are rich. And they've earned the right to every Lifestyle luxury they purchase. It is the effort to maintain the lifestyle that creates economic tension for these high-income professionals.

Many of them live with the uneasy awareness that if they can no longer do the work—if they die or are disabled, either temporarily or permanently—the ride is over. The lifeblood dries up and the lifestyle drains any reserves this breed of Lifestyler may have accumulated.

By using Wealth Builder principles, professionals can position themselves to maintain their economic freedom by focusing on investments instead of possessions. Even so, few have the enterprise-building experience that births the most successful of all Wealth Builders, the Enterprise Capitalist.

decisions about the use of company resources. These businesses never quite gel because employees compare their compensation with what they imagine the owners take home; their hard work isn't about building a successful business or even raising their standard of living. It's about building an owner's McMansion or buying a Lexus for the owner's family. Loyalty and commitment drop. When ownership's personal material needs come at the expense of the needs of the business, the financial health of the business is at risk. Ironically, Image Lifestylers often find that keeping ahead of the Joneses means running faster and faster on the treadmill. They lose their quality of life. And building wealth is rarely a byproduct of these choices.

In extreme cases, Image Lifestylers' organizations end up feeling like dysfunctional families. Lifestylers keep the numbers of the business to themselves; if their players knew how much revenue was coming in, they rationalize, employees would believe they deserve a bigger share. These owners' malcontent leaders keep an eye out for better opportunities; turnover is high across the board. Lifestylers' businesses are often divided into camps, with energy poured into "getting mine."

Image Lifestylers look affluent on the outside; they might even believe they are. But most extreme Lifestylers owe more than they own; more than they can comfortably cover some months. They intend to pay it off soon, maybe next year at tax time, if they can wangle a refund.

The impact on the lifeblood of a business is profound. Money is squandered. The business is not viewed as an asset to be invested in, so it is unlikely to cross the chasm that separates the businesses that subsist from the ones that are true wealth machines. If the business does by some chance reach extraordinary heights, the pinnacle is precarious. The financial underpinnings of the company rest on the shoulders of an Image Lifestyler who measures success in personal harvest, not the long-term good of an enterprise with a life of its own.

The single greatest cause of missed opportunities for building wealth in the 21st Century is the Lifestyler mindset.

Building Wealth, Building an Asset

How do Lifestylers compare to Business Wealth Builders?

By contrast, Business Wealth Builders view themselves as stewards of valuable assets. They make choices and decisions that increase an asset's market value. They are willing to defer financial rewards while a business finds its legs because they take the long view. They know the day will come when they have earned the right to reap the rewards and provide generously for their families' comforts.

Until that day, Wealth Builders live comfortably, not lavishly. Neither their homes nor their vehicles are symbols of wealth; they buy what they can afford without depleting personal or company funds. At the right time, they may earn the right to a home overlooking the lake

Lifeblood Plus
Profile of Wealth Builders

Wealth Builders:

- Recognize that the business is the wealth-generating machine behind their financial portfolio

- Measure the success of the business based on earnings, net worth and potential for passive income generation

- Live comfortably, not extravagantly

- Earn the right to grow

- Measure use of resources against ROI

- Firewall personal & business finances

- Know how to multiply money, not bury it or consume it

- Maintain low debt-to-equity ratio

- Reinvest portion of profits to grow the business

- Protect cash as the lifeblood of the business

or the golf course, if the purchase is a prudent investment. They took the kids to Europe last year; this year they'll spend a week camping. Their college funds are secure, or at least in motion. They strive to give their families as much of their time, energy and attention as they give their businesses, even though that balancing act is hard—sometimes impossible in the early stages—to maintain.

Wealth Builders constantly reinvest capital strategically to grow their business. As a business grows, they earn the right to new equipment, new facilities, new locations. They carefully calculate what portion of capital should be invested in developing smart and talented players who are going to use those smarts to build valuable assets that are independent of ownership—unlike Lifestylers who are wrapped around

---

Lifeblood Plus
Profile of Lifestylers

Lifestylers:

- Equate success to image, possessions, reputation, power or freedom

- Know how to leverage assets to yield maximum cash

- Count on tomorrow's harvest to balance the financial equation

- Accrue debt to make purchases without realizing they are liabilities, not assets

- Place great value on having the latest and greatest technology or equipment, without calculating ROI

- Fund everyday expenses with debt as a regular practice

- Keep others in the dark about financial information

- Model an entitlement mentality

- Look at top-line revenue to gauge financial health

- Wonder where the money goes

---

the axles of their businesses. As their business asset matures, they look for opportunities to diversity their financial portfolio beyond the business.

Wealth Builders measure their success at least in part by the success of their people, in much the same way a parent watches with pride—and certain misgivings—as a child becomes less dependent. They clearly see the day when their assets will run without them, when they can exit if they choose. If they exit, their businesses still provide a dependable source of income; or they may achieve a valuable exchange of stock for capital. Their future-minded orientation means they may see themselves investing in other enterprises because they love the entrepreneurial quest.

Every year, their businesses become more valuable and that abundance spreads to leaders and employees and to their communities.

The Wealth Builder trades on the promise and potential of tomorrow to weather challenges and make smart choices today.

Owners Speak

"My ego doesn't drive a Lexus."

Eric Lerner
Action Plus
Sportswear & Specialties
Founded 1992

The impact of these choices on the lifeblood of the business is profound. Cash flow is king. The business asset gains true market value. It attracts talented players and strategic allies who have the ability to drive ever-higher levels of success. When the business reaches critical growth junctures, capital planning pays off with readily available investment capital from trusted sources.

The Wealth Builder versus the Lifestyler. Neither is wrong. But every owner needs to make a conscious decision, and not a decision by default, because the choice determines where your entrepreneurial journey ends up. Which path are you on? Is it leading you where you want to end up?

Which mindset is better?

Your answer only matters if you aspire to achieve economic freedom. The choice is yours, as long as you understand that answering by default won't result in the prudence and the disciplines required to build business wealth.

That's not a value judgment. It is simply an observable phenomenon, proven over and over again in the world of business ownership.

The choice does, however, reflect our root beliefs about business ownership.

The world view of the Lifestyler is: ***This is my business. It's here to serve my personal objectives.***

The world view of the Wealth Builder is: ***My purpose is to build something with the potential to create significant wealth.***

There is no wrong choice or right choice. But I do offer a caution: We can't play the Lifestylers' game and expect the Wealth Builders' results.

Am I biased in favor of the Wealth Builder? Of course I am. My life calling is to work with business owners who have chosen to build a great enterprise and serve as stewards of their resources. My bias isn't about who's wrong or right. It's about concern that too many entrepreneurs

Lifeblood Plus

Not everyone desires to be a Wealth Builder. For some business owners, creating the lifestyle they want is satisfying enough. Some work from home or do the thing they love without worrying about marketing or revenue projections or strategic planning. Some work long enough to sell the business and retire to the beach. Others enjoy the power and prestige that come with playing the part of the wealthy entrepreneur. Every business owner gets to decide for himself what path he wants to be on. Nobody has the right to judge that. But the Lifestyler is choosing to play a game in which few will harvest because they don't play by the rules that can win the Business Wealth game.

Lifeblood Plus
Are you a Lifestyler or a Wealth Builder?

Score each statement on a 1-5 rating, with 1 being Strongly Disagree, 2 being Disagree, 3 being Undecided, 4 being Agree and 5 being Strongly Agree.

- When I make decisions about spending company resources, the priorities of the business come before personal or family priorities.

- My business is more of an investment than it is a place to work or to express myself.

- As the owner, I'm accountable to the leaders of my company regarding my compensation and the decisions I make about using company resources.

- I openly share critical financial information with company leaders and key employees.

- Company leaders and key employees know their compensation structure assures financial rewards when they achieve specific goals that increase revenue or the equity value of the business.

Here's what your total means:

1-5: You're a Lifestyle Owner to the extreme. The lifeblood of your business is threatened by your decisions and your actions.

6-10: Don't kid yourself. Your Lifestyler decisions may not be causing problems yet, but they will catch up with you.

11-15: It's Big Decision time: What do you really want from your business? Your inconsistency causes fear and uncertainty in your company.

16-20: Your instincts are good; you're likely a natural when it comes to wise decision-making around money. But you aren't yet living up to your tremendous wealth-building potential.

21-25: Congratulations! You have the mindset of a Business Wealth Builder. Persevere in your journey.

risk missing out on the significant opportunities of the 21ˢᵗ Century. Because of an often unconscious choice, they are risking their economic freedom.

MONEY EQUALS FREEDOM

Business owners come through my door dazed because they've realized that they're running out of time and they're running out of money. The lifeblood of the business is drying up and they have no idea why. The reasons are often complex, but can most often be traced back to a single choice, a choice many have made unconsciously.

They've been playing the game like a Lifestyler and not like a Wealth Builder.

The name of the Wealth Builder's game is Protect the Lifeblood, which provides the raw material for building significant wealth. That game is played by Smart Money Rules.

Most of us don't realize we've been playing blind until we begin to smell failure. Cash flow slows to a trickle. The new business pipeline is empty. We're starting to sweat. We look around our organizations and wonder how we can let our people down when they depend on us for their livelihood. Sitting around the dinner table, we obsess about saving enough money to get the kids through college. We look at ourselves in the mirror every morning and think, "What if I fail? What will I do? What *can* I do?"

Money equals freedom. And these owners are under high threat of losing theirs because they didn't protect the lifeblood.

Remember Donnie, the guy in Chapter 1 who had the boat and the plane and the multi-million dollar company? The business was temporarily cash-strapped, so he went to his bank to borrow enough to carry him over the hump. The bankers, you'll recall, told him he was virtually bankrupt. He was out of cash and out of time.

Because of his long history of success, Donnie was able to negotiate with the bank. He got the money he needed. But from his cash-poor position, Donnie had no leverage with his banker. The bank held all the cards and when Donnie walked out with the money he hoped would save him, the bank was in control of his business. Until he started playing by a different set of rules, Donnie worked for the bank.

Playing by Smart Money Rules doesn't mean you'll never need outside capital. It doesn't mean money will never run short. It doesn't even mean that your business is guaranteed to succeed. But Wealth Builders know that following the rules positions them to take maximum advantage of the significant wealth opportunities of business ownership.

Owners Speak

"I see people who have success, start to see some money coming in and all of a sudden they start buying new houses, bigger cars. They overspend in their personal life by taking it out of the company and that doesn't allow the company to grow. I can remember plenty of times when Jeff and I couldn't pay ourselves in the beginning. If you take out too much too early you don't have the investment to be able to grow and do things that you've got to do. That's a big mistake. Guys want to live at a level beyond where they're truly at."

Eric Hillman
Europa Sports
Founded 1990 200 employees

Clearly, business is about money. It is the key to our existence, the measure used by the marketplace to score our game. When we have money, we survive to play the game one more day. The future is still ours to determine. When we run out of money, we've run out of time. When we've run out of time, we've run out of choices.

We've run out of freedom.

How do we avoid squandering our wealth potential? How do we win the game and secure our own economic freedom? The answers lie in our choice to play by the same rules as the Wealth Builders. Our choices could make us one of the almost 600,000 businesses that close their doors every year. Maybe we'll be satisfied with moderate success. Or maybe our choices lead us down the path to building extraordinary enterprise wealth.

The right choices for each of us lie in our ultimate vision of the business: What do we really want? And is it propelled by a powerful purpose?

Ownership Perspective

1. Have you chosen to make it a priority to pursue a lifestyle or an enterprise legacy through the means of your business?

2. How do you see the entrepreneurial revolution changing the face of America's economy? What implications does this revolution have for your business wealth opportunity?

3. What is your view on harvesting the rewards of your business versus investing in it as an asset?

THE WEALTH BUILDER'S CODE

*The vision of building a
meaningful legacy unlocks the wealth
potential of an enterprise.*

Chapter Three
Your Vision, Your Money

"It takes a vision of something greater than money in the company coffers to inspire others to pull the plow."

Times of great change present tremendous opportunity for significant economic gain. This time of Entrepreneurial Revolution is one of those times.

Most will squander the opportunity because they've never thought, in deliberate terms, about their wealth-building choices. The Lifestyle Owner makes choices that seldom yield the full wealth potential of the business asset. Mindset: *This is my business. One of the reasons I started a business is so I could call my own shots. That's the way the game works.* This mindset follows unspoken rules that few of us question.

Becoming a Business Wealth Builder implies a different choice. It implies that an owner has decided to build something besides a money machine. It implies that an owner has decided to build something of significance. Therein lies a critical difference in mindset and beliefs between the Lifestyler and the Wealth Builder: The Wealth Builder operates out of the vision of a business growing purposefully toward significant goals.

Until we as owners make the decision to build out of purpose, passion and significance, we may get rich but we will never build significant business wealth. The lifeblood of our business thrives on a rich, compelling vision.

ROOTED IN PURPOSE

Walter and Hank thought they owned a woodworking company. They thought their purpose was building and installing custom cabinetry in schools and other institutional settings. They'd founded the business in the mid-90s after becoming disillusioned with the business where they were sales reps. After a half dozen years, their balance sheet looked pretty good for two successful salesmen. They had a solid client base and a good reputation in the industry.

But they felt restless. Often, they were at odds because they weren't always on the same page with their decision-making. They seemed to pull in different directions and the company felt the strain. Sometimes they asked themselves, "Is this all there is?"

These two guys went on retreat to figure out what should happen next. They believed the retreat would help them determine whether expanding into another state was the right move. Or whether they should restructure their compensation model. Maybe it was time to settle the push-pull of two distinct business entities under their corporate umbrella. On retreat, they would make some tough decisions.

They came back from retreat with the drawing of a tree on a flip chart page. They came back with a unified vision in the form of a Mind Map.[6]

"I think we were a pretty classic case of multiple owners who couldn't seem to agree on anything," Walter says. "I wanted to build a big enterprise. Hank was happy as long as he could take home a healthy paycheck and enjoy relationships with our customers. How in the world did we expect to get anywhere with all of us heading in fundamentally different directions?"

At times, these two partners felt so far apart in their ideas that the business seemed in danger of breaking apart.

So they packed up and headed off to the Chalet Club with my partner Paul and me to figure out what happened next. They were a little surprised at what did happen next: Paul and I asked them to describe their vision for the company, to

do some blue-sky dreaming about what their company could become if there were no limits. What did the summit look like for this company they were building together? How would the business be different when they reached their ultimate goals?

Now, guys like Walter and Hank aren't really into the soft stuff. Blue-sky dreaming has all the earmarks of soft stuff. No, these guys want to know about money. About ROI. About revenue and overhead and cash flow. They didn't have this term to use at that time, but they were into the lifeblood of their business. Vision? Come on, Sam, get real.

Being good sports, they played along when I persisted. They talked about franchising or acquiring a smaller competitor or developing different segments of the market—a multitude of possibilities. They began to zero in on the ideas that resonated with both of them. Walter started writing everything down on a flip chart, showing how one thing branched off from another, how it all linked to roots of experience and customer satisfaction, with a taproot that was superior craftsmanship. Before long, the lines and circles and arrows on the flip chart transformed into the drawing of a tree, a tall, mature oak with plenty of room to branch out and anchored by deep roots.

When they came down from the mountaintop and returned to the office on Monday, they taped that drawing to the wall in their cramped meeting room. They made sure every key employee in the business experienced that drawing. They explained every branch and every root and helped people see where they fit in the company. When they hit walls and faced the inevitable challenges, they looked at the

---

Lifeblood Plus
Mapping Your Vision

Vision can be limited if we define or describe it without exploring our dreams. So creating Vision begins by igniting the thinking process. Here are the guidelines for touching off your imagination:

Identify Core Values: Defining Vision begins with passion for an idea, as well as a deep sense of purpose. What are you striving to achieve? What are the beliefs and core values that drive you? Look for the key words that resonate.

See the Future: Translate the beliefs, the values, the excitement, the purpose into changes, actions, results at some point over the horizon. Allow the beliefs to take shape. Think symbolically about beliefs, values, goals.

Commit it to Paper: Write it down. Create symbols. Draw pictures. Refine it. Shape and sharpen the idea. Make it both concrete—the company will have four distinct divisions—and abstract—customers will value our commitment to their needs.

Articulate it to Others: Take the Vision to others, express it with all the power and passion you have. Tell them how you will move from the present to the future, and bring them with you.

---

tree to remind them what the struggle was about. They had a visual representation of the vision that united them.

They did expand into a new state. They did break apart the two divisions into separate companies. They did make some tough decisions that have resulted, three years later, in significant progress for the company, including building a new facility for their expanding enterprise. They did it all with a clear understanding of where the move fit in their vision and how it contributed to the flow of the lifeblood through the living organism of their business.

Walter and Hank learned that their purpose as business owners went deeper than building cabinets.

UNLOCKING THE WEALTH POTENTIAL

If you're a business owner, you have a vision. We all do. If we didn't, we'd be pushing paper or pounding nails for somebody else, checking off the days till payday. But vision serves many purposes in a business.

- It inspires people to follow us.
- It helps us survive challenging times.
- It gives focus to our decision making.

Here's the most important purpose vision serves:

Vision unlocks the wealth potential of our companies.

A clearly articulated vision that drives the business toward accomplishments that are loftier than economic gain is actually the foundation on which economic gain rests. Vision gives people an itinerary and a roadmap for the destination they're striving toward.

Here's an example of what I mean. A friend in my community who owns a service business has had a hard time sustaining success. She struggles along, then nails a big contract and thinks she's arrived at a sustainable pinnacle. She doesn't consistently attract high talent and when she does land talented players, she can't hang onto them. The pipeline doesn't deliver another big contract in a timely fashion, the boom goes bust and she struggles again until she nails the next big contract.

Now, there are no doubt a number of reasons my friend can't make the business cross the chasm to build enterprise wealth. But one of them I know for sure: She's never communicated a significant vision to her organization, so they've filled in the blanks for her. From their perspective, the owner's vision goes something like this: "If you all work hard, one day I'll own a home in the mountains."

Guess what? Nobody goes the extra mile for that.

I know my friend has a greater vision. But she hasn't recognized the significance of that vision in driving the wealth-building engine. How does vision unlock the wealth potential of a business? Here's what the pathway looks like:

Vision
↓
Belief
↓
Commitment
↓
Priorities
↓
Choices
↓
Habits & Disciplines
↓
Results

Vision enables others to see goals and accomplishments that are worth working hard to achieve—worth sacrifice, even. When people see and **believe** in the vision, they are willing to make a **commitment** to do what is needed to make the vision a reality. Once people have committed to achieving certain goals, identifying the right **priorities** becomes more clear. And focusing on those priorities gives clarity and decisiveness to the **choices** that become the consistent **habits and disciplines** that drive the right **results**.

Owners Speak

"I never fully understood the role vision plays. I always thought I was supposed to get a consensus from everybody in the company about the vision and it never worked. When it became clear to me that it's the owner's vision, I had to go inside to get clarity around what I truly saw in my own heart. Once I did that, it was easy to drive through my leaders."

Tana Greene
StrataForce
Founded 2002

One of those results will be economic gain. But it takes a vision of something greater than money in the company coffers to inspire others to pull the plow. Some of us just haven't given much thought to what our vision is. We haven't dug deep to get past the obvious—*I want to make a lot of money*—to the substantive, like making a difference in the world or improving life conditions for others or doing something better than it's ever been done.

Yet every day we make dozens of decisions that impact the vision and the lifeblood of the business. When we know our vision we'll know the pathway to follow to achieve our ownership objectives. We'll know whether we want to be a Lifestyler or a Wealth Builder. Then we can make the conscious decision to play the game by Smart Money Rules.

And that's a decision any business owner can make and benefit from. We don't have to be a Wealth Builder to play by Smart Money

Rules. Playing by Smart Money Rules can result in financial health. And that's a fundamental we can all believe in.

Ownership Perspective

1. Do you believe there is an inextricable link between the owner's vision clarity and enterprise wealth?

2. Do you have a compelling vision that sets the stage for enterprise wealth? If not, why not?

3. Do the leaders in your business understand your vision?

PART TWO

SMART MONEY RULES

SMART MONEY RULES

1. *Learn to Earn*
2. *Eyes on the Money*
3. *Make Cash Flow*
4. *Avoid the Debt Sinkhole*
5. *Hedge Your Bets*
6. *Leverage Down*
7. *Think Like a Capitalist*

PART TWO

SMART MONEY RULES

Because of my work and because of my passion for entrepreneurship, I spend my days shoulder-to-shoulder, toe-to-toe with men and women who are in the trenches of the Entrepreneurial Revolution. I see their points of brilliance and I see their minor misfires and their colossal screw-ups. They tell me the secrets even their spouses don't know, much less the other business owners in their circle of friends and colleagues.

And as I walk with them on their journey, I find myself wondering about the difference between the owners who are making it and the ones who aren't. Their walk and their talk don't seem so very different. But the winners at the enterprise game must know the secret. They must've cracked some kind of secret code that separates the ones who never quite make it from the ones who make it really big.

These business owners—the one-gun slingers and the freedom seekers, the entrepreneurs who crossed the chasm and the ones who hit the canyon floor—taught me the rules that allow the Wealth Builder to succeed while the rest struggle. The rules that enable Wealth Builders to wind up with a healthy business when their product is no better than ours. I've cracked the code Wealth Builders follow and I've distilled seven key concepts around money—the Smart Money Rules.

The seven Smart Money Rules are:

1. **Learn to earn.** Embedded in Wealth Builders' consciousness is a keen sense of profit. If it doesn't make a profit, it isn't a business asset, it's a liability. If we want the business to serve our needs, we must first serve its needs by learning how to earn a profit. The key to profit is tied to four concepts covered in Chapter 4.

2. **Eyes on the money.** Wealth Builders know the three measures of healthy finances and how to stay on top of them in about ten minutes a week. Master that discipline and gain clarity about the single most important tool for taking control of your enterprise in Chapter 5.

3. **Make cash flow.** We love revenue and we love profit. But Wealth Builders' understanding of and respect for the link between money and time keep the door open. Understand why and how to keep the cash flowing in Chapter 6.

4. **Steer clear of the debt sinkhole.** The lure of debt is a silent killer—business owners often don't realize their financial health is endangered until it is too late. Wealth Builders understand: a) how easy it is to slip into debt and how hard it is to crawl out of debt; b) the difference between good debt and bad debt; c) how to develop a debt strategy; and d) how to maintain the upper hand with your lenders. All are covered in Chapter 7.

5. **Hedge your bets.** Business is risky, but Wealth Builders have an instinct for hedging against the odds and avoiding over-exposure in the risky decisions that must be made every day. Wealth Builders keep their options open while narrowing their assumptions, a practice covered in Chapter 8.

6. **Leverage down.** Getting stuck in the entrepreneurial mindset of creation and innovation blocks Wealth Building. At certain life stages of the enterprise, we must create, we must hunt and we must innovate. Other stages ask us to elevate up and out

of the organization, to regain perspective on the big picture and focus on the vision. At other stages, it is time go deep into our companies to tap sources of "capital" that are easily overlooked. In Chapter 9, learn how we can heighten the awareness of the gold right under our noses and leverage it to increase the value of our business asset.

7. **Think like a capitalist.** This final Smart Money Rule is the most significant one of all because it represents the first stage of life as a Wealth Builder. At this stage, Lifestylers slam into their awareness of the barriers they've created to building wealth. Although they may have found ways to apply the first six Smart Money Rules, this one typically brings them face to face with the limitations they've placed on the business. In fact, this Smart Money Rules points to a significant crossroad for every owner who desires to build Business Wealth. It is a bridge to the practices that lead to true business wealth. Both money and opportunities are lost every day by business owners who fail to anticipate the needs of a business on the brink of significant success. Chapter 10 explores thinking like a capitalist in order to navigate this crossroad in order to achieve the fullest equity potential of a business.

Of course, playing by the Smart Money Rules isn't the end game for committed Wealth Builders. The game is complex. But the first step in cracking the Wealth Builder's Code is to play smart with company finances. From the basics—which are so fundamental that some of us fail to appreciate the complexities—to the practice of capital planning—a practice that few master and many stumble over—Smart Money Rules equip us to elevate our game.

Whether you have Lifestyle objectives or Wealth Builder aspirations, protecting the lifeblood of a business leads to more money for achieving any owner's objectives. Playing by Smart Money Rules protects that lifeblood.

SMART MONEY RULE #1
Learn to Earn:

Business wealth is not measured by revenue; it is measured by what's left over at the end of the day.

Chapter Four

Smart Money Rule #1:
Learn To Earn

*"Let me be the first to deliver the sad news.
No profit equals no business."*

Want to know how successful you **really** are as a business owner? Look at it through the eyes of a capitalist.

Through that lens, here's the main question you'll want to answer: What's the return on investment?

Of course, a capitalist wants other answers, too. Is it a viable business model? Is there a consumer willing to shell out money for your product or service? Is it scalable? A capitalist isn't impressed that you're working yourself to death, putting in 60 to 80 hours a week, paying yourself below market value. In fact, the shrewd capitalist might see those

---

[2] Names and details of business owners and their companies have been modified to preserve confidentiality, except where indicated with full names and/or company names.

dubious badges of honor as signs that you haven't learned the most basic lesson of ownership: how to earn a profit.

A couple of years ago, I walked a potential investor through a number of our client businesses[2]. A young capitalist, Mark Maier was looking for opportunities to put his money to work making more money.

We visited a young business that had been phenomenally successful as it moved out of Start-Up and into the Growth stage of its development. A high-end residential remodeling company, it had ridden the crest of the rising tide of a move-up and relocation boom in a Sunbelt city. Dot-com optimism and boomers who had reached the peak of

Owners Speak

"We opened in 2001, so 9-11 hit us hard as a new business. They say that whatever doesn't kill you makes you stronger. I think in our case, that turned out to be true. We learned how to survive in a tight market, how to continue to provide services our customers could afford and needed. I'm not sure we would have learned those lessons any other way. If we'd started in the middle of the IT bubble, I'm not sure we would be as strong a company as we are today."

Dave Griffin
ProfIT/CS
Founded 2001

their earning potential spurred a renovation fever. The company's sales crew didn't even need sales skills. Sales strategy essentially involved putting a sign in the yard of a house in an upscale community and waiting for neighbors to pick up the phone. This company could barely keep up with the hunger for Tuscan-style kitchens with imported stone, utility sinks and handpainted murals, master baths that recalled the luxury and pampering of resort spas, and bonus rooms with surround-sound and stadium seating. Waiting lists for renovations were months long. Extravagance was in, it came with a price and nobody seemed to mind writing the check.

Then 9-11 hit and hit hard. The shift in the marketplace registered 6.9 on the Richter scale for companies that had raked in revenue during the boom. And despite all the money that had flowed in when times were flush, this company was limping. The boutique renovation company with no sales strategy needed an infusion of cash to wade out of the rubble and rebuild.

So Mark Maier came in to take a look. Mark is an investor and board member for one of my businesses. He'll tell you he learned the principles of wealth building by watching his dad, Willy, build wealth in a start-up. Touring this company, it didn't take long for Mark to decide that his hard-earned capital wouldn't be funneling into this business.

What did he see that made him reach that conclusion?

He saw excesses. While riding the crest, this young company had renovated and lavishly furnished its own high-style facility in the old-money side of town and sank cash into fully-loaded SUVs for its estimators and crew chiefs—all of which would bring pennies on the dollar if ownership reached that point of desperation called liquidation. Mark saw the Rolex on the owner's arm and the desperation in his eyes. He took it all in. He'd seen similar facilities and similar looks of desperation in the aftermath of the 9-11 attack and when the dot-com boom went bust.

What else did he see? Poor financial disciplines. Debt piled upon debt. A mindset that having the money to pay the bills this week meant the business was doing okay.

How would an infusion of outside capital be used? To pay debt and avoid going under one more week, one more month, one more year. Mark's hard-earned money wouldn't be used to make more money because it was all needed for the rescue operation.

This business, Mark knew right away, wasn't operating out of earnings, and probably hadn't been even when the business was a money machine.

How could it? The owner knew how to churn, but he had never learned to earn.

PROFIT LINKS TO CASH FLOW

Mark had no need to learn—or play by—Smart Money Rules. Decades earlier, his dad founded and led an Erie, Pennsylvania, company to stability and sustainability.

===

Lifeblood Plus
Myths about Profit

As savvy as we business owners are, our heads are often full of fantasy about the money of our business.

- We think the value of the business asset is measured by its top-line revenue.

- We think if we work hard the money will take care of itself.

- We think capital equipment equals a valuable business.

- We think a brilliant innovation delivers profit.

- We think having enough money to pay the Overhead Monster must surely mean we're profitable.

The Wealth Builder knows those are all false assumptions. And false assumptions will kill you.

_____

Willy Maier founded Omni Plastics in 1979, when the plastics injection molding company where he served as chief engineer sold out to a major corporation. Willy was offered a position with the corporation, but he had no desire to be swallowed up by a bureaucracy. Omni Plastics was born. As all founders must, Willy worked harder than hard and weighed every move against the bottom line and squeezed every dollar for the highest return he could get.

After earning his MBA, Mark could have enjoyed living like the crown prince, keeping a low profile and living off the profits and figuring he was set for life and, after all, wasn't that the whole point. But Mark had no desire to run the company. He had no interest in squandering his dad's hard-earned wealth, either.

Investing money to *make* money is Mark's interest.

Mark became a classic angel investor. He's been successful because he learned what it means to earn instead of churn by watching his dad's moves, his decision-making process, the guiding principles that made Willy Maier a successful capitalist to his own enterprise. Mark says, "My dad's fiscal conservatism was ingrained in me from birth. It's different for me, coming into a successful business as a second-generation owner. I don't have to be as conservative as Dad had to be, building it from scratch.

"But I watched what Dad did and I learned to recognize people who play smart with their money and the ones who don't. I learned to know the difference."

Mark grew up watching his dad protect the lifeblood of the business. That focus on the lifeblood of the business and the smart moves that keep it flowing made Mark a hard-nosed capitalist who can walk into a business and know instinctively whether an owner has learned to earn.

For Mark, a good investment is all about ownership that understands *using* money to *make* money.

WHAT'S LEFT OVER?

The good venture capitalist understands the delicate economic balance in every business. This tricky balance is maintained by paying attention to a simple equation.

How much comes in?
How much goes out?
What's left over?

Too many of us measure our success solely on the answer to the first question. *How much comes in?* A hundred grand in sales revenue the first year? *Whew! Dodged the bullet.* A quarter million? *Good. We're hanging in there.* One-point-five? *Great!* Ten million? *The sky's the limit!* But the Wealth Builder has learned that paying attention only to the first question—how much comes in—won't keep a business afloat for long. In today's economy, an enterprise can get turned upside down in a heartbeat if ownership equates churning revenue with being profitable. Failing to pay attention to the whole equation might not kill a business today or even next month. But revenue alone—even spectacular revenue—won't keep a business alive and healthy for the long haul.

Remember, it's the lifeblood that keeps the business alive.

Lifeblood isn't solely about what comes into the business. It's also about what flows out of the business, and the timing of the flow in and out. The lifeblood must flow. Not clot. Not hemorrhage.

Lifeblood Plus
The Laws of Great Enterprise

The first requirement for learning to earn is having a viable business model, which leads to a healthy economic formula. A robust business model follows certain laws that aren't optional. I think of them as the Laws of Great Enterprise. How does your business stack up?

1. The Law of Market Niche. Do you provide a product or service that is highly desirable to some clearly identifiable segment of the marketplace?

2. The Law of Unique Brilliance. Have you found your company's unique fingerprint in the market? Do you know how your company rises above others in the marketplace? Do you consistently operate out of that giftedness?

3. The Law of Customers. An enterprise is as healthy as its relationship with customers. Is your customer base healthy, balanced and loyal?

4. The Law of Profit. A business without a profit is not an asset—it is a liability. Do you demand to know the return on investment in every key use of time and money before you pull the trigger? Or do you fire and pray?

5. The Law of Optimization. Optimization is a fancy word for making the best use of resources to achieve the best possible results. Are your company's resources of money, time and talent applied strategically and effectively to achieve specific goals and outcomes?

Flow.

Learning to earn means paying attention to all parts of the financial equation that ultimately add up to profit. One of the key measures of healthy lifeblood is profit. But too many business owners don't fully understand the complexities and the delicate balance that make up profit. Here's one way the Wealth Builder measures profit:

> ***Profit is the portion of revenue that is available for uses above and beyond the day-to-day needs of the business.***

When you've written checks to pay for materials and supplies, what's left?

After you've paid the rent and the phone company and the payroll, what's left?

When taxes have taken a bite, what's left?

When you're current with every monthly obligation, what's left?

What's that? There's nothing left, except maybe a little red ink?

Then let me be the first to deliver the sad news. No profit equals no business. In start-up, you may shoestring the operation for a time while you catch up with profitability. At key junctures, you may forego healthy profit to fund the right growth moves. But over time, like a heart with blocked arteries, the business will starve from clogged cash flow. Every limb and organ of the business will deteriorate from lack of lifeblood.

> ***Without profit to support positive cash flow, you don't have a business, you have a potentially dangerous liability.***

Maybe you have an enjoyable entrepreneurial pursuit. Or a hobby. At worst, you have a liability. No profit, no business. And without a viable business, of course, nobody's building any wealth. And if we're not building wealth, we're just another employee with the glorified title of Owner.

If we want the business to serve our needs, we must first serve its needs by learning what it takes to earn a profit. Learning to earn can be boiled down to mastering three key focal points:

1. Knowing the numbers.
2. Selling it right.
3. Managing costs.

Suddenly, business ownership is slightly more complicated than just finding somebody who'll pay us to do what we love and cashing the check. Playing by Smart Money Rules—the only game that pays off in wealth building—demands mastering those three focal points.

Lifeblood Plus
Curbing Cash Loss

Cash-loss factors are different for every company. But if we pay attention to three specific strategies we can begin to impact our cash problems: 1) a capital strategy, 2) a pricing strategy and 3) a strategically-timed collections and payables strategy. For some types of businesses, a fourth category where significant cash is lost is inventory management.

Minimize the impact of growth with a capital strategy. Business owners are bullish and we're often afflicted with that uniquely American malady, Bigger is Better. More money, more customers, more products, more territory, more services—surely "more" will solve our problems. But growth without a capital strategy can put unexpected strain on resources. Overhead goes up, the need for equipment or inventory goes up, mistakes come with a higher price tag. Growth can gobble up cash. (For more on developing a capital strategy, see Chapter 10.)

Minimize the potential impact of high service, low margins with a pricing strategy. My long-time partner, Paul Bennett, never tires of reminding business owners that "the fastest way to go out of business is to position on service and sell on price." Yet today's market conditions seem to demand that we ignore the fundamental correlation between our profit margins and the level of service we can afford to give our clients and customers. We struggle with the realities of a marketplace

1. Know the numbers. Maybe you have all the numbers at your fingertips, or in your head. You know the sales figures from last month or even last year. You know the big-ticket items that make up the bulk of your overhead. But how many of *these* numbers do you know:

- What's your break-even in sales revenue?
- What are your fixed costs?
- What is your gross profit percentage?
- If you sell different lines of goods or services, what is the gross profit margin for each?
- What are the total cash obligations you must pay each week or each month, including the nickels and dimes that soon add up to hundreds and thousands?
- What kind of revenue can you realistically expect given the dynamics of your industry or niche?

---

that buys on price but expects concierge service as part of the package. A faulty pricing strategy can keep margins so low that it's impossible to develop a profitable business.

Minimize the impact of an anemic balance sheet with a focused collections and payables strategy. Here's a critical intersection of time and money. When money comes in slowly and goes out rapidly, it creates a cash crunch. When we allow accounts receivable to extend one day beyond industry standards, we open the door for our customers to erode our cash flow. We're letting our customers use our money interest-free. We may also operate with a hair-trigger payables policy—it's not due until the 15th, but we write our checks on the 1st; if so, we're letting our vendors use our money interest-free. We're choosing to be a cash flow victim. The answer is to negotiate the best terms on both ends, manage collections so that we get our money on time and avoid paying vendors earlier than required.

Minimize the cash tied up in unproductive inventory. This is another area where the relationship between time and money is apparent. The goods sitting in your warehouses are unproductive; you can't bill for them so they are costing you money. The longer they sit there, the more they cost you. Libraries have been written about inventory control. But simply stated, get it in and out the door as quickly as your industry allows.

Gaining a comprehensive picture tells us 1) what kind of numbers are probable within our industry; 2) what kind of numbers we require to fulfill the basic needs of the business; 3) what our ideal economic formula looks like; and 4) how our actual performance stacks up against what's probable and what's required.

Does the reality of our particular niche in our particular industry allow for healthy economics? If so, by making sure we know our numbers daily, weekly, monthly, we can then calculate and recalculate the numbers over time in order to move in the direction of our ideal formula.

So whether we are striving to reach profitability for the first time or working to elevate to the level of profitability that allows for wealth building, knowing the numbers is the most basic requirement for achieving profitability.

Knowing our numbers means **understanding what the numbers are telling us.** If we haven't studied all those numbers and plugged them into an equation that shows us where the business really stands, we

---

Lifeblood Plus
Seven-Minute Drill

I can tell in seven minutes whether an owner runs his business by the numbers by asking these questions:

1. Do you know the average revenue for the last three months?

2. Do you know the average profit for the last three months?

3. What do you project for the next three months?

4. How much money do you have in the bank?

5. What are the balances and aging of your accounts payable and your accounts receivable?

6. What is your monthly break-even?

7. Do you know the profit margin on every product/service you offer?

---

don't know the numbers. We're just playing with them. Until we understand the numbers, we don't know what conditions we need in order to serve our clients *and* make a profit. We have to know the numbers.

2. Sell it right. Maximizing revenue potential is a first step in achieving the numbers in our ideal economic formula. Getting to the right numbers on the sales side of the equation entails:

- Selling the *right product or service*
- Selling at the *right price point* to achieve the *right profit margins* to achieve a healthy balance between volume and profit
- Selling to the *right customers* under the *right terms* and conditions to improve cash flow and/or minimize working capital needs

Right product, right price point, right customers —it's a balancing act. Too often we make some of these decisions by default or by focusing on one element—the price we want, for example—and not all three.

Sometimes it's easy to see the effects of faulty pricing strategy, but hard to trace the effects back to the root problem. A local landscaping company was in high-growth mode a few years ago. Word was spreading that Andy's crew served the production home builder better than anyone else. He was signing up business in the next county and the next state; business was hotter than hot. Every morning when his trucks hit the road, Andy saw dollar signs.

What he didn't realize was that he was watching those dollar signs wave goodbye on the way out the front gate.

The business kept rolling in but every month the books looked a little more anemic. How could the company be doing more business and making less money? It just didn't add up. Andy's frustration grew. Was the bookkeeper miscalculating? Was somebody stealing from him?

Well, yes. In fact, Andy was stealing from himself every time he signed a contract.

"I finally realized we were still pricing the jobs like we did when they were five miles away," Andy said. "Revenue was up, but travel costs were killing us."

Developing a pricing strategy means understanding all the factors that impact the cost of delivering the product or service, then paying attention to those factors.

3. Manage costs.

Most of us remember the days of the efficiency experts. They were seen as the solution to managing costs by finding ways for us to yield the same results for less dollars. There was good value in that, and there

---

Lifeblood Plus
Selling It Right

Selling it right isn't one decision. It's a series of decisions that will ultimately help us achieve the right product or service, the right price and the right customers. To get the right answers, ask the right questions at every step.

1. Are we offering the product or service we're best-suited to deliver in terms of capabilities and quality?

2. Are we willing to work outside our sweet spot in order to close the deal?

3. Are we cultivating the customers/clients who are likely to be with us for the long haul?

4. Is this customer base able to pay the price we need in order to be profitable? Do we know what the market will bear?

5. Does this customer consistently deplete our time or energy with demands that are above and beyond the parameters of our terms?

---

still is. But in today's world, containing costs requires the discipline of prudent decision-making linked to a thorough knowledge of our economic equation (knowing our numbers).

High on my weekly work plan is containing the cost of goods, the cost of sales and the expenses of overhead. At every turn, we need to know: How much is this going to cost? Are there hidden costs that will come back to haunt us? Raw goods, labor, transportation, equipment, administration, supplies, facility—dollars spent in every area potentially represent dollars we could've saved.

It all starts with a detailed budget. This isn't a lesson in budgeting; we can all find plenty of sources to help with that. But we need to remember that Wealth Builders are rigorous and disciplined in their budgeting practices.

Here's what the budget does for us: enables us to track expenses every month and compare those numbers to the numbers projected in the budget. If they're different—and they often are—we must

Is that because customer terms are too vague or unstated? Have we failed to create conditions for success?

6. Can we create the efficiencies of scale that are necessary for healthy profit margin with this product/service and these relationship terms?

7. What will we trade off if we choose to step outside our area of giftedness, or serve the customer who diverts us, or live with margins that starve the business? Will the price be market share? Standards of quality? Efficiencies? Maybe the failure to focus means we don't get quite as good as we could be?

8. Can we live with these trade-offs for a season in order to bridge the gap to the next stage of healthy growth?

9. If these compromises become our company's modus operandi, is it possible that the business fails to gel?

10. How likely are we to build business wealth if we make these trade-offs beyond the short-term?

understand why. Answering "why" pinpoints the problems and points toward the solutions.

I'm known in my business for scrutinizing every nickel we spend. I know that nickels add up to dollars and dollars add up to hundreds, which compound and build wealth. For every expense—that includes rent and payroll and marketing—I ask myself how it connects to revenue and whether it will deliver some kind of return. I keep overhead low. I link compensation to measurable performance. I walk the razor's edge of healthy profit margin, trying not to shortchange clients by giving too little or giving them Neiman Marcus service for Wal-Mart prices.

Containing costs is certainly far more complicated than squeezing pennies. It requires vigilance and a willingness to be accountable for decisions around money. But do I squeeze pennies? You bet I do, whenever possible. Most importantly, I try to squeeze them where it makes the most sense.

We'll never make a fortune squeezing pennies; but if we don't squeeze them, we can lose it all.

Lifeblood Plus
Leaving Money on the Table

The money we leave on the negotiating table comes right off our bottom line when it could be a shot in the arm to the lifeblood of the business.

Sometimes the sales team is more motivated by closing the deal and getting the commission check than they are by getting another $25 or $2500 on the deal. Granted, that doesn't sound like a big deal. Looked at another way—from the owner's perspective—that extra cash would be pure profit.

Depending on our product or service, the money left on the table might look small. Only a quarter per widget, for example. But if we sell a million widgets a year, those quarters add up to $250,000. Maybe our sales total ten a month and the price is such that a hundred bucks doesn't seem like much. But if we leave behind $250 on each deal, that's $30,000 a year.

RETAINED EARNINGS

Learning to earn seems elementary. If we work hard, surely the money takes care of itself.

Wrong.

Then surely we can count on our accountant or our bookkeeper—our CFO, for Pete's sake, look how much we're paying him!—to pay attention to the numbers.

Wrong.

We're the owner. It's our job. Others may be diligent. But nobody else will ever care as much as us. No one else will ever have as much on the line as we do.

At its most basic level, learning to earn means weighing every decision against its impact on the lifeblood of our business. For every dollar used to serve customers and keep the doors open, Wealth Builders ask: Is it necessary? Is it enough? Is it too much?

Learning to earn isn't about being miserly. It's about **retained earnings**—earnings that aren't obligated to run the business, but available for other choices that can create wealth. If we can't retain it, we haven't earned it. Business Wealth is built only on what is retained.

Ownership Perspective

1. Do you think "profit" all the time?

2. What would a smart capitalist say about the potential investment opportunity of your business? Should his answer have some impact on the way you, as a stockholder, look at your business?

3. Do you measure the success of your business by the earnings of the company or the size of your salary?

SMART MONEY RULE #2
Eyes on the Money:

Never assume that anyone else will pay attention to the money. Only the owner has enough at stake to be constantly vigilant.

CHAPTER FIVE

Smart Money Rule #2: Eyes on the Money

"Are your eyes on the money?
If not, how can you be sure that you're making any?"

More than a dozen years ago, I was learning Smart Money Rules the hard way as the owner of a company with factories, warehouses, trucks and expensive capital equipment. We looked healthy. Orders were coming in, product was going out. We were beginning to come out of the nosedive the company had been in when I purchased it a few years earlier for the cost of a good used car.

Still, cash was hard to come by. So hard to come by that sometimes we just didn't have any. But it seemed to me that we were juggling the bills pretty successfully, figuring out the drop-dead dates for the ones that **had** to be paid and holding the ones that could wait until our customers paid us. Nobody seemed to be sending collection agencies after us, so I assumed I was playing the money game pretty cleverly.

Owners Speak

"I had to learn to keep my finger on the pulse of the company's finances instead of waiting until month's end to find out where we stood. Money is our biggest fear and when we don't keep our finger on the pulse, we make bad decisions because we're making them out of fear, not good information. When I wasn't continuously monitoring the money, I always found myself asking, 'Where's the money?' We were at $10 million, $15 million, $20 million and all I could think was, 'Where's the money?' If you take your finger off the pulse, it will bite you and that bite is always in the pocketbook."

Tana Greene, Co-founder and President
StrataForce
Founded 2002

One day while rushing down the highway to a customer appointment, I picked up my mobile phone to prep for the meeting with my VP. But when I dialed his number, I found myself talking to someone from the mobile phone company. I was confused and irritated by the distraction. The customer service rep said, "Our records indicate that you haven't paid your bill."

Insignificant details. I was on big stuff. I tried being reasonable. "I need to make this call."

"I understand," the person from customer services said, equally reasonable. "But we need to get paid."

Now I was indignant. "There must be some mistake."

The only mistake, as it turned out, was my failure to keep my eyes on the money. I had no idea we were behind in our accounts payable, especially in lifeline services like utilities. If I'd been paying attention, I would never have been blindsided. The lifelines of the business would never have been starved of their lifeblood.

WHERE THE BUCK STOPS

Maybe you've been in similar predicaments, blindsided when a credit card was declined at a business lunch or an impatient landlord cornered you in the elevator. How do we get so out of touch with the money of our businesses?

That's easy—it takes courage to look at the money. Finding out how tight the money really is can be discouraging. And our relationship with money is typically wrapped in fear and ego. We're afraid of being vulnerable if people learn how much we don't know. We're afraid of losing control and losing face.

Besides, that's somebody else's job.

Don't we pay good money to bookkeepers for the very purpose of making sure the bills get paid? We've got smart people all over our money—accountants, CFOs, financial advisors. Why aren't they taking care of us? After all, we didn't go into business to count money. Most of us don't love spending quality time with our spreadsheets.

Dale is pretty typical of owners of small manufacturing companies. What he really likes is selling, building relationships with key accounts. And that's working out pretty well because the company has been successful enough to have others who run the equipment and schedule production and manage distribution.

Lifeblood Plus

The Flash Report can be used in any business, but is critical in emerging businesses or Gazelle businesses where growth is rapid and cash is volatile.

He sat in my office, sweating over a cash crisis and swearing over the irresponsibility of the bookkeeper who had allowed the crisis to happen. She should've *done* something.

As it turns out, she *had* done something. She'd gone to Dale weeks earlier, warning him that a cash crunch loomed. Maybe he was too anxious to listen or too overworked to take the time. Whatever the case, Dale told her, "Not now. I don't have time for that today. I'm busy trying to earn a living."

When insufficient revenue caught up with Dale, the bookkeeper took the heat.

Here's a little-known fact for every business owner who prefers the head-in-the-sand method of cash management: Bookkeepers do not manufacture money.

Owners like Dale feel blindsided and betrayed and self-righteously indignant when they're caught with their eyes off the money. And it happens to all of us. Wealth Builders, too, have had their share of unpleasant surprises around money. The hard lesson they've learned is that ownership is always accountable for monitoring the money.

Wealth Builders keep their eyes on the money.

DOWN AND DIRTY

Keeping our eyes on the money isn't rocket science. It doesn't take hours and hours. It doesn't even require a special affinity for numbers or advanced training.

In fact, it takes me about 10 minutes once a week.

I'm not a CPA. I wanted something simpler than poring over a balance sheet and trying to calculate what it was telling me. So, like the classic entrepreneur, once I saw the need, I figured out a better and more efficient way to do it. I've identified a process that gives me a weekly one-page look at the current state of certain financial metrics of my business. I've structured these down-and-dirty financial reports in

---

Lifeblood Plus
Eagle Eye

Wealth Builders who keep an eagle eye on the money:

- produce and review financials monthly;

- organize financials around revenue, gross profit, cost of goods sold, general administration/overhead and net profit;

- dissect revenue streams using separate profit centers within the business for the purpose of pinpointing opportunities and threats;

- use financial statements to track money trends using monthly, quarterly and annual comparatives;

- work with an external board of advisors who understand and focus on company financials.

---

a way that reveals the key information clearly and quickly. So quickly, in fact, that I call it a Flash Report. In about the time it takes to review and sign checks each week, a well-constructed Flash Report gives me a real-time financial snapshot of the business, including short-term cash flow trends from the previous week.

The other vital financial tracking tools are the income statement and the balance sheet.

The balance sheet gives me an accurate monthly picture of my cash balances, my payables and receivables balances and the amount of debt I owe. It tells me the accounting net worth of my business (a different measure from the market net worth of my company) each month.

An income statement is a basic scorecard on critical performance indexes of the business—revenue, gross profit, key expenses and net profit.

This reads like Money 101 for business owners, I know. And it is. But for Wealth Builders, this is anything but elementary. They view these commonplace financial reports through a different lens. They aren't just making sure the bills

Lifeblood Plus
1-2-3 Financial Reporting

1. Flash report: a down-and-dirty weekly report on key financial metrics of the business

2. Income statement: a monthly overview of cost of goods sold, overhead and net profit

3. Balance sheet: an accurate scorecard of retained earnings and the equity position of the business

get paid and the customers don't get too far behind. They use financial reports to take care of the short term while planning for the long term. Wealth Builders make a discipline of reviewing financial reports and piecing together a comprehensive picture. Financial reporting is the source of the insights they need to make prudent decisions around the use of the company's lifeblood resource of money.

A system of monthly financial disciplines and a thorough knowledge of how to interpret and use them put the business owner in control of the engine that drives wealth.

FOLLOWING THE MONEY TRAIL

Taken together, I use financials to spot problems before they become crises, to make adjustments that can improve the numbers and to arrive at informed decisions. I can track sources of revenue. I can set prices with this information; establish budgets; react more quickly to changes in the marketplace; pinpoint problems earlier.

Here's the trail of money I follow:

Top-line revenue: I look first at the income statement for last month's revenue. This is an important number and I pay close attention to it. But taken in isolation, top-line revenue can lull me into a false sense of security. I never celebrate until I follow the trail to the end, where I learn whether there's something left over.

Revenue sources: If all the revenue goes into one pot, I'll miss key information about the financial picture of my company. When my companies have multiple sources of revenue, I need to know how

Lifeblood Plus
The Flash Report

One of the first tools we provide for our clients is the Flash Report, a customizable document designed to give them key financial information each week. The particular categories of information might be different for each business and each owner.

Some of the metrics a Flash Report might contain include:

- Cash balances

- Receivable balances

- Payables balances

- Receivables aging

- Line of Credit (LOC) balances

- LOC availabilities

- Customers who are most significantly past due

each income stream is performing. The definitive application of this principle leads to the actual break-out of business units, each with its own budget, revenue and expenses. But even the simpler process

Lifeblood Plus
Sample Flash Report

FOR PERIOD ENDING:	6/7/2002	

BANK ACCT BALANCE	Current	Last Flash
OPERATING	22,533.90	172,865.88

ACCOUNTS RECEIVABLE		
TOTAL	1,617,705.86	1,545,240.93
0-30 DAYS	754,388.34	899,970.00
31-60 DAYS	641,987.26	377,950.61
61-90 DAYS	163,801.15	185,083.32
OVER 90 AND INELIGIBLE	57,529.11	82,237.00
TOTAL	1,617,705.86	1,545,240.93

ACCOUNTS PAYABLE		
TOTAL	147,086.43	147,086.43
0-30 DAYS	20,479.66	20,479.66
31-60 DAYS	20,968.32	20,968.32
61-90 DAYS	51,275.29	51,275.29
OVER 90	54,363.16	54,363.16
TOTAL	147,086.43	147,086.43

LOAN BALANCE		
TOTAL	920,408.00	1,057,565.00
AVAILABILITY	322,642.00	108,716.00
BALANCE TO TOTAL A/R %	57%	68%

SALES			PRIOR YEAR
WEEK TO DATE	179,104.73	192,059.36	177,246.00
YEAR TO DATE	4,114,370.64	3,967,284.21	5,834,945.79
HOURS BILLED	15656.87	15983.77	
# OF CLIENTS BILLED	27	26	
GM %			
% TO GOAL			

OFFICE #851	OFFICE #852	OFFICE #854	TOTALS
FTE = 5	FTE = 4.5	FTE = 4.5	14
GM$ =	GM$ =	GM$ =	
GM$ per FTE =	GM$ per FTE =	GM$ per FTE =	
STATUS:	STATUS:	STATUS:	

of tracking different revenue streams tells me where revenue is being generated and how much is being generated in each area. Broken down this way, the income statement tells me where the organization is underperforming or missing opportunities. It gives me information that I can use for strategic decision-making about where to invest the resources of my company.

Cost of goods sold: Now I'm inching up on the truth about my numbers. What does it cost to get a product or service out the door and into the hands of customers and clients? Supplies, materials, equipment, maybe delivery, sometimes labor, sales expenses—all the hard costs that are absolutely necessary to produce a product or service must show up on the income statement. Now I'm beginning to understand what I need to do more of and what I need to do less of.

Gross profit: This is where I draw conclusions about all the numbers I've reviewed. What's left when I subtract cost of goods sold from top-line revenue in each profit center? Is it enough to support a healthy business? The true story of the company's financials begins to emerge.

Overhead: Financial guys call it G&A, or General and Administrative. Most business owners just think of it as the necessary evil of overhead: what does it cost to support the business of the business? If overhead is a four-

Lifeblood Plus
The Money Trail

Examine your weekly, monthly, quarterly or annual financial statements in this sequence to understand the status of your cash position and your profits.

Top-line revenue
↓
Revenue sources
↓
Cost of goods sold
↓
Gross profit
↓
Overhead
↓
Net profit
↓
Cash flow
↓
Trends on the spreadsheet

68

letter word for some business owners, it's only because of how easily it can snowball. When I deduct this number from the gross profit, it takes me to the next number in the money trail.

Net profit: What's left over to work with when it's all said and done? Without net profit, I can't make improvements or growth moves. Over the long haul, this number tells me this machine's potential for building wealth.

Cash flow: Does it? Or is the trickle so slow that the only way to get by is to tap lines of credit? Is the flow dammed up with accounts receivable that are aging beyond the terms of our agreements? Could be cash flow has become a real gusher, spewing out money the minute it comes through the door. Cash is king and if it isn't flowing in faster and more steadily than it's flowing out, I have a problem. Maybe I need to set better customer terms. Maybe I'm too aggressive with payables. Maybe I need to pay more attention to my clients' satisfaction level. Maybe I need better collections procedures. My minimum goal is to fund the business on each month's cash flow. I can't know if that's possible until I've examined the whole picture. One payoff for funding the business on cash flow, not sales revenue or debt, is that I pay closer attention to the business's highest priorities when it's time to allocate resources.

Trends on the spreadsheet: This month's numbers are important. But taken out of context they may not provide me with the real story. I drop the numbers into a spreadsheet that allows me to compare this

Owners Speak

"If you ask my people they will tell you I know what each restaurant is doing without ever being there. Up until I had 11 restaurants, I kept folders in my Jeep. I had all my receipts. I could show you what every location paid for lettuce. Even today, I can tell you how many French fries we sold last month within five orders. With today's technology, I could be on an island in Greece and access any of my restaurants and tell you whether table number 5 has been bussed. I don't have to be there to keep an eye on the cash register."

George Couchell, Founder and Owner
Showmars Restaurants
Founded 1982; 800 full-time employees

month's numbers with last month's and last quarter's and last year's. That spreadsheet makes it easy to see the trends that tell me where the business is headed. Sometimes I recognize opportunities we can capitalize on. Often I spot problems before they go on too long and become crises. This month's information is important; the long view of the broader picture is critical.

That's the money trail I follow. How about you? Are your eyes on the money? If they aren't, how can you be sure that you're making any?

The first time I reached a quarter of a million dollars in revenue in one of my early companies, I had no idea how to read financial statements. No idea what depreciation was. No sense of financial ratios or retained earnings. All I understood was accounts receivable and cash on hand and how much I owed. If I can learn to follow the money trail, anyone can.

It takes courage to look that unflinchingly at the business's finances. But it's not an option if we're playing the Smart Money game.

Lifeblood Plus
Accrual vs. Cash Accounting

Cash accounting recognizes revenue when it is collected and expenses when they are paid. Modified cash accounting recognizes certain non-cash expenses such as depreciation.

Accrual accounting recognizes revenue when it is earned and expenses when they are incurred.

Accountants generally consider accrual accounting to be a more accurate picture of the business's profitability at any point in time because it accounts for all of a company's transactions, whether or not money has changed hands.

Here's the danger for the owner who's following the money trail: money that is earned but never collected negatively affects the cash flow. And if we use projected revenue for decisions about the use of capital, we are operating with funny money. It's real money, when we have cash in hand.

Wealth Builders know instinctively what the flow of money in and out of the business looks like from one week to the next—but they don't rely solely on instinct. They make a point of following the money trail so they know exactly what's been billed, who has paid and who hasn't, when more is going out than they have coming in. Cash is the lifeblood of the business. Wealth Builders know that and pay attention to it as if it were a life-or-death matter. Because it is.

Ownership Perspective

1. Do you have fears about money that make you take your eyes off the money?

2. When you think about the checks and balances to protect the lifeblood of the business, do you feel secure?

3. Who really knows the numbers of your business? Do they care as much about it as you do?

SMART MONEY RULE #3
Make Cash Flow:

Cash flow is the vehicle for turning the source of financial health—revenue—into the fruit of our financial health—profit.

CHAPTER SIX

SMART MONEY RULE #3:
MAKE CASH FLOW

"Cash is hard to get hold of and harder to hold onto. Its nature is to flow right through our hands, an always moving target."

When I was ten years old, my best friend Joey was the richest kid I knew.

Joey had a paper route. Some might not view that as the most lucrative vehicle for a savvy entrepreneur. But Joey could always fund a trip to The Shake Shop, so I knew he was rich.

Everywhere Joey went, he carried a blue book, his official paper route ledger. Whenever we were overtaken by an overpowering craving for ice cream, Joey would pull out his ledger, knock on a door, smile engagingly and tell his customers that it was time to collect on their subscription. Whoever answered the door would hand over a few dollars and we'd go buy a quart of ice cream.

Could be that was when my desire to be an entrepreneur was born.

One Saturday, I learned the lesson of not paying attention to cash flow. I'd spent the night at Joey's and we were getting ready to launch into our weekend. Then Joey heard someone at the front door and got a funny expression on his face.

"Mr. Carson's here," Joey said, dropping his voice to a whisper. "Let's hide."

Owners Speak

"Cash flow gets 90% of entrepreneurs. The most important thing is to be on top of your receivables and that's unpredictable. People assume clients are going to pay them in 30 days and if they don't, they're not well-positioned to adapt and handle it. People have to cushion their receivables and prepare for the worst case."

Bob Confoy
HomeGuard Inc.
Founded 2003

Mr. Carson was the manager of the paper boys. He'd come to collect for Joey's route. The money Joey had collected from his customers, of course, had already been used to purchase other necessities. So Joey and I hid behind the couch and listened to his mother and Mr. Carson unravel the truth about Joey's cash flow management issues.

I didn't hang around for the meeting with the capitalist who bailed Joey out of his financial difficulties. The last thing I heard as I hightailed it out the door were the ominous words, "Wait till your dad comes home."

That was my first real lesson in the dangers of confusing revenue with profit, and the cash flow problems that can follow.

A MOVING TARGET

What, exactly, is cash flow?

The very words describe our dilemma. Cash is hard to get hold of and harder to hold onto. Its nature is to flow right through our hands, an always moving target.

In trying to gain a clear picture of the dynamics of cash flow as a major component of the lifeblood of a business, I've come to realize that cash flow isn't a definable thing as much as it is a process. A process, by the way, that looks and operates a little differently in every business.

As owners, we tend to focus our obsession on three main money categories: revenue, profit and cash flow. They tend to fuse in our thinking. Revenue is down, so of course profit will take a hit and we're bound to run into a cash flow crunch. In actuality, these three financial metrics are interconnected but completely separate measurements of our financial health.

And one of the problems we, as owners, create with the lifeblood of our business is that we tend to be biased in favor of one metric or another. The key to robust lifeblood is the main artery that connects 1) the source of financial health—**revenue**—and 2) the management of our financial health—**cash flow**—and 3) the fruit of our financial health—**profit**. Remember, a portion of our revenue always streams into paying expenses. Profit is the portion we get to keep. At that point profit can either be harvested or it can remain in motion as the raw material from which wealth can be built.

To put it succinctly, revenue moves into the cash flow process and, if the flow is successful over the long haul, a portion of it may become profit.

If cash flow is a process, when does it begin, when does it end and what happens in between? How do we protect that process so it can best result in the end product of profit?

Lifeblood Plus
Working Capital

Working capital is the portion of every dollar of revenue that must be reinvested to produce a new dollar of revenue. Here's how to figure it.

Current assets
(assets that will convert to cash over the next 12 months)
minus
Current liabilities
(payables plus debt that must be paid in the next 12 months)
equals
Your working capital

Trickling In, Gushing Out

For most businesses, the cash flow process begins the moment we can bill a customer or client. The cash flow process continues through the point of collection, and concludes when some or all of it funnels into working capital. If anything is left, we call it profit.

Sounds pretty straightforward. But we all know how many variables are at work within that process.

First, do your billings always go out on time? Mine don't. No matter how hard we work at it, things get in the way. Somebody has to pick up a sick kid at school. Holidays happen. The billings go out late.

Lifeblood Plus
The Cash Flow Quiz

How would your leaders answer the following questions?

- When profits are down, do you have the information necessary to know whether to raise prices or cut costs?

- Do you know which of your company's products or services are the most profitable?

- Are you investing resources in products that don't contribute positively to the bottom line?

- Are your profit margins healthy? Does your pricing structure allow you to give good service and still make a profit?

- How long will it take to achieve a return on investment in a new product or project?

- How much of your budget is fixed overhead and how much of it is variable overhead?

- Do you carefully dissect the costs attached to production so it is possible to track indirect costs such as transportation or delivery?

- When you plan key moves or major initiatives, do you calculate the impact across the organization when calculating ROI?

Second, is there sometimes a lag between the verbal agreement and the signing of a contract? Maybe the guy who has to sign is out of town or somebody forgets to deliver the contract. I'm certainly guilty of letting that happen. But it's only a few days. How bad can that be?

Do customers seem to think that "payable on receipt" means they are supposed to take a couple of weeks to stroke a check? What do your collections procedures look like? Does the money get to the bank before the close of the banking day or does another day get added to the process?

Our Chief Financial Advisor calls all these seemingly minor delays the hidden days in the billing cycle. In the best case scenario, hidden days may number only a couple of days. In the worst case, we could be looking at a couple of weeks. Their impact is major.

Of course, while all those little glitches are slowing down the flow of money in, what's happening to the flow of money going out?

Lifeblood Plus
The Story of Lifeblood

The story of the lifeblood of your business is found in following cash as it flows through your company, from point of contract to collection. That story begins with the sale and the negotiation of terms that allow for favorable cash flow and continues through every system and process in the business. The speed and efficiency with which money moves from the first billable day through collection and ultimate deployment—that is the lifeblood story.

Do your employees forego payday when the admin's kid goes home from school sick? Not at my company. Is the payment on your term note for capital equipment due on the same day every month even when your client is out of town and can't sign checks on time? Maybe the purchasing clerk wants to cross something off his list and orders materials two weeks early. The money is going out on time whether it's coming in or not. So cash may be trickling in on one end and gushing out at the other.

But, hey, it's just a few days. Right?

Cash flow is a sensitive metric. Even the smallest change can have huge impact on cash flow.

Perry's company is a $16 million business, a service business that was healthy enough to acquire one of its competitors a little over a year ago. On any given day, this company's accounts receivable ranges from $1.7 to $1.9 million. By shortening collection time by **one day**, this business stood to realize up to $45,000 in additional cash flow every quarter.

Perry was stunned as he contemplated what he could accomplish by freeing up an additional $45,000 every quarter. Needless to say, the next day he set changes in motion.

We're not all looking at receivables in the millions. But wouldn't it be interesting to know how improving our collection time by a couple of days might impact the flow of cash through our business?

And shouldn't we all know about certain factors that drive the cash flow of our business and what those factors are doing to the lifeblood of our business? Improving these cash flow drivers typically results in a high return with a relatively low investment of resources. The three cash flow drivers are:

- Accounts receivable
- Inventory (when applicable)
- Accounts payable

Clearly, the impact of these drivers varies from business to business. Retail, for example, is almost never affected by accounts receivable but is certainly impacted by inventory. A service company won't be dealing with inventory headaches but typically struggles with aging accounts

Owners Speak

"I'm a hands-on money person. It's one of my daily tasks to make sure to have enough cash in the bank to allow us to take on big projects when they come along. Our cash management plan is that we have $100,000 on hand so we can finance ourselves when the big projects come along."

Eric Lerner
Action Plus
Sportswear & Specialties
Founded 1992

receivable. And the more narrow your margins, the less room you have for poor cash management and the greater the potential for significant impact. Every business could improve its cash flow by increasing efficiencies in one or more of these areas.

FOCUSING ON THE PROCESS

Business owners get testy when cash flow is anemic. Some of us try to fix cash flow problems by tearing people's heads off. While that may seem satisfying in the moment, I don't think I've ever seen it solve the problem. That isn't to say that the people of your organization aren't a part of the solution.

Making cash flow king in our enterprise requires getting our leaders focused on making the necessary changes that support and improve cash flow drivers.

1. Use weekly flash reports to keep all eyes on the money. (See Chapter 5 for a sample flash report.)

Owners Speak

"Sometimes I feel like a CPA without a license. We have 25 or 30 jobs going on at the same time and you have to make sure a job is billed out as soon as it's finished. Sometimes you have to make 27 phone calls to collect on one account. I spend the majority of my day maintaining cash flow."

**Linda Holden
The Linda Construction Company
Founded 1982; 57 employees**

Lifeblood Plus
Retail cash flow

Inventory and accounts payable are the cash flow drivers in retail. Cash flow begins either at the time of the sale or at the time you must pay for the goods, whichever comes first. So you can easily fall into a pattern of operating with a negative cash flow if you don't have the clout or the negotiating skills to establish favorable terms with suppliers and wholesalers. Steps to improve the cash flow drivers will be vastly different from one establishment to another with most solutions being customized..

2. Set concrete objectives for improving key measurables and make someone accountable for each objective.
3. Build systems, procedures and an action plan for achieving each objective.
4. Clearly set cash flow terms with customers, with contracts and systems to support and reinforce those terms.

Remember, ownership models the standard for keeping the company's mindset on money. Your leaders will follow your example of understanding the way cash flows through the business and the ripple effects most of us overlook.

In the story of the lifeblood of your business, cash flow is king. If revenue can't be processed and managed efficiently enough to produce the end product of profit, the lifeblood of the business will never be robust. As business owners, we're only as good as our ability to affect cash flow as the vehicle for carrying the lifeblood of our business.

Ownership Perspective

1. What is the hardest part of your role of keeping your company's cash flowing? Who can and should help you share this burden?

2. In your personal life, are you a spender, a saver or an investor of your money? Do you treat the resources of your business like you do your personal resources?

3. How would your decision-making change if you really believed that every decision you make in the business impacts the flow of your money and the wealth potential of your business investment?

Smart Money Rule #4

Avoid the Debt Sinkhole:

When we gamble with debt,
the stake is our freedom.

CHAPTER SEVEN

SMART MONEY RULE #4:
AVOID THE DEBT SINKHOLE

"The borrower is servant to the lender."

What's your boat worth to you? Your Lexus? Your house on the lake?

Are they worth your freedom?

I've seen owners make choices about badges of success that put their freedom at risk. Most of them had no idea they were jeopardizing their businesses for the sake of a shiny new toy.

At our core, most business owners are freedom seekers. We don't want anyone else to control our destiny. When I talk with business owners about their original impetus for becoming entrepreneurs, the most common theme is freedom.

Without realizing it, we trade our freedom for symbols of the lifestyle of the rich and powerful. That is the fast track to debt. And debt is a slippery slope to loss of freedom.

I know, I know. Debt is the American way. It's a given. Kids get credit cards before they've worked a day. Tomorrow's leaders walk away from college with a degree and a mountain of debt. When we max out a credit card, we find another provider. And business owners finance tomorrow's dream with today's debt.

If easy access to debt is a cornerstone to our cash flow planning, we're building our business on quicksand.

SLAVES TO DEBT

The first time I met Nancy was at her home in an exclusive neighborhood of 6,000 square foot homes where most folks had rooms full of designer furnishings and a boat docked at the private marina.

Nancy had called me to talk about her business, so I was on task. We went straight to her home office—a fully stocked bar was nearby and the lake was visible from the picture window—so we could talk about the pain of the business.

The pain came down to this: She had lost her freedom. She wanted it back. But she was so buried in debt she saw no way out.

Nancy had paid with her freedom for the trappings of a certain lifestyle. The debt monster demanded to be fed, even at the expense of her health, her marriage, the stability of her business. She had become a slave to her possessions. More than once, Nancy said to me, "I'd sell everything I have to get my freedom back."

She had learned the hard way how easy it is to get into debt and how hard it is to get out of debt.

Today, Nancy doesn't live in that house. She owns her home outright in a more modest neighborhood. Her life is simpler, with fewer trappings. She lives debt free.

Owners Speak

"Debt is something I'm very comfortable with as long as it is debt that propels the business forward so that you can retire that debt in an appropriate time frame."

Rudy Alexander
The Elevator Channel
Founded 2001; 18 employees

When I met Nancy, she was a Lifestyler. Today she is a Business Wealth Builder.

GOOD DEBT, BAD DEBT

Don't get me wrong. Debt has its place. Many of us, as early-stage entrepreneurs, needed to jump-start our businesses with some degree of debt, which we usually secured with our own collateral, the promise of future stock options or a promissory note. At that stage, I've certainly said to myself, "I've got to do this to stay in the game."

At all stages, debt may be a reasonable alternative for capitalizing an opportunity to take the business to its next level—expanding a facility that would otherwise impede growth or upgrading equipment that no longer keeps pace with industry standards or hiring the player who will elevate your game. That's appropriate use of the tool of debt.

The standard to use when gauging whether you're contemplating good debt or bad debt is ROI. Will there be a return on the investment? What will the ROI be? When can you expect an ROI?

If the answer to those questions doesn't justify the expense and the added price tag of debt, don't kid yourself. This debt isn't financing an investment.

Debt becomes a sinkhole when we use it to dig our way out of a

hole we've already dug. When we're using it to buy time to avoid tough decisions about layoffs or other cost-saving measures. When we can barely afford the payment, but have all the confidence in the world that we're holding the winning lottery ticket. When we have no idea how we'll ever get it paid off. When the cost of losing is too high. That's bad debt, waiting to swallow you up.

Inexperienced entrepreneurs who view debt as just another way to pay the bills are especially susceptible to runaway debt. Entrepreneurs who haven't yet sweated over payroll month after month often don't fully respect how hard it is to make the real money necessary to pay for using the funny money. Credit cards, once a rite of passage or a hedge against the unexpected, have become an expectation and a convenience.

Calculated use of debt is one of the practices that make experienced entrepreneurs disproportionately successful as second- and third-round owners—they've often seen the sinkhole up close and personal. They know the risks firsthand and they've learned to watch their step around debt.

The dot-com implosion illustrates what can happen when easy debt is used by inexperienced entrepreneurs who have never learned to earn.

About a decade ago, I was lunching with a young dot-com entrepreneur, high on the vision of his future as a multimillionaire. He had sought and received a ton of investment capital. To him, that equaled a successful business. I suggested that his future hinged not on how much money he could raise but how much money he could earn

Lifeblood Plus
Good Debt/Bad Debt

Good debt	*Bad debt*
Capital equipment that will provide a return	Latest & greatest technology
Facilities for growth	Office image
Key player acquisitions	Employee loans
A roll-up acquisition	Cars for owner's kids.

by developing a service or product people were willing to buy at a price that delivered a profit.

"You're living in the old economy," he told me. "Wake up and join the future."

He's busted now. He had to learn the hard way that being able to borrow capital didn't equal being able to earn a profit.

I vacillate between feeling vindicated and feeling regret that I couldn't convince him that investment capital, received and handled too offhandedly, could easily become just another form of debt that could pull him under. The rules of the old economy are as valid today as they were 50 years ago.

Lifeblood Plus
Rules of the Old Economy

The six best rules our parents knew about debt:

1. Set aside 10% of every dollar earned. No exceptions.

2. Live within your means.

3. Pay your bills on time.

4. Earn the right to invest in growth.

5. Secure a profit in every transaction.

6. These rules never change..

STAYING AFLOAT

When facing the debt decision, today's choices may determine whether the bank is running your show tomorrow. What can we learn from business owners whose freedom has been buried under debt?

Diving in is easier than climbing out. Business owners typically attract lenders who have incentive to give us debt. It's so easy, and so tempting, to say "yes" to five or six figures. Let's not forget why all those lenders want to loan us their money: when we do, we work for them. After Uncle Sam, the next slice of every dollar we earn goes to our lenders. A piece of wisdom from the book of Proverbs tells us, "The borrower is servant to the lender." Always has been, always will be. The Wealth Builder knows that we work for the lender until the debt is paid off. That makes the borrower the employee and the banker the boss. No wonder the biggest buildings in most cities are financial institutions. *I owe, I owe, so off to work I go.* No thanks.

Use debt for the sure thing, not the gamble. Pursue untested concepts with earnings, not with debt. Risks are inherent to building enterprise. But the riskier the move, the more fiscally conservative we should be in financing it. Wealth Builders earn the right to make bold moves. They fund with debt only when they have an ace in the hole.

Never use business debt to serve a lifestyle. This doesn't mean we can't reap rewards of our hard-won success. When the business can afford to reward us—and the other players who have made the rewards possible—we should reap some reward. But Wealth Builders know that lifestyle can be a bottomless pit. If lifestyle becomes our priority, no matter how much we buy today, it won't be enough to satisfy us tomorrow. And lifestyle never pays dividends. So when we finance it with debt, we're waving that money goodbye.

Develop a strategy for paying off debt. Too often we sign on the dotted line, cash the check and only think of the debt once a month when we make another payment. Borrowed money should make possible increased profits that not only boost the bottom line but also provide the money to repay the debt. If debt only allows us to stay above water today, all we've done is dig a deeper sinkhole. To stay afloat when we borrow, we need a realistic plan for repayment, starting by resolving the circumstances that led to the need for debt in the first place.

Always operate from strength. Business owners make the critical mistake of waiting until they need money before they try to secure it.

Owners Speak

"For the first twenty years, I didn't borrow much money at all. When I did, it was 90-day notes and I paid them off in 90 days. If I could afford to open a restaurant I did and if I couldn't, I waited. It's a slow process, but consequently, the business built a solid foundation."

George Couchell, Founder and Owner
Showmars Restaurants
Founded 1982; 800 full-time employees

Bankers and other capitalists have no respect for need. Need is weak and they aren't eager to invest in weakness. When you go to lenders in times of financial famine, terms will be structured overwhelmingly in their favor and you'll pay dearly for whatever crumbs they're willing to risk. The Wealth Builder understands cash needs well in advance by forecasting the numbers, anticipating capital needs and lining up the resources while the company looks fat. Establish lines of credit whether you need them or not. Establish them even if you have no intention of tapping them.

Let me tell you about a Wealth Builder I know who understands how to use debt to improve his financial position and give the banks a run for their money at the same time.

Ed's about three years into a start-up. He has a small staff, a small office, a small client base. And a big line of credit.

When he first opened his office, Ed went to the bank where he's been doing business for years. Over the years, he's made a point of getting to know all the bankers—and the people they report to—by their first names. So the decision makers he approached were like old friends; they trusted him and knew he had always proven to be a good risk. He outlined his plan for them and asked for a line of credit.

Lifeblood Plus
The Smart Money Debt Strategy

- Always operate from strength.

- Use debt for the sure thing, not the gamble.

- Never use business debt to serve a lifestyle.

- Develop a concrete strategy for paying off debt.

The bankers were impressed. He didn't need their money and bankers love to give their money to people who already appear to have money.

Ed, they wanted to know, *what's your collateral? Should we use your house?*

Lifeblood Plus
Banking Buddies

I love the fairy tale that we can make friends with our bankers and thus write our own ticket when the time comes to borrow. Maybe that still happens in small towns. But in many markets, the players in banking come and go quickly. So the banker relationship you cultivate today may not exist next week. Only at the top will you find more stability. That's where to spend your energy building relationships..

No, that wasn't really what Ed had in mind. Ed wanted to separate the business finances from his personal finances. Couldn't he guarantee the line of credit with his signature? After all, they'd known him for years. He'd always paid what he owed, when he owed it. If that didn't work for them, well, it wasn't like he needed the money. Maybe he'd just wait.

So, of course, the bankers established a line of credit for Ed. Bankers will loan money all day to people who play hard to get.

A few months later, Ed went to another banker he'd met through one of his clients and took out a loan. He used that loan to pay off the line of credit, which improved his standing with the first bank. Some time after that, Ed began to build a relationship at a third bank. Eventually, Ed had unsecured lines of credit totaling $250,000 available to him whenever he needed it.

"I didn't need the credit," Ed said. "I just wanted to create a little elasticity in my available credit. Every time I paid off a loan or a line of credit, my bankers increased the credit available to me. They were actually competing for my business."

Sometimes Ed even uses the money his bankers are so eager to lend him. But only when he knows exactly how his finances are going to line up in the near future to allow him to pay it off. And only when the money is being used to make his company better in some way.

Ed's business is immature in many ways. But Ed shows all the earmarks of a Wealth Builder in the making.

Wealth Builders learn the right times and the right reasons to go into debt, as well as the right strategies for handling debt. Debt doesn't have to be the enemy if we make calculated choices instead of desperate, reckless or uninformed decisions. In fact, when viewed as a bloodline providing flexible access to liquid capital, debt can be a significant part of a Wealth Builder's capital plan.

It's not prudent or reasonable to declare that we should avoid debt at all costs. But failure to manage it strategically is a significant threat to the healthy flow of the lifeblood of our business. And remember, when you gamble with debt, your freedom is at stake.

Ownership Perspective

1. Where are you vulnerable to becoming mired in debt?

2. When in your life have you learned firsthand the painful lessons of debt and exposure? How have those lessons affected the way you treat debt today?

3. What safeguards do you have in your life to insure against bad money decisions?

SMART MONEY RULE #5
Hedge Your Bets:

*Every failure traces
back to a false assumption.*

CHAPTER EIGHT

SMART MONEY RULE #5:
HEDGE YOUR BETS

"Unsupported guesswork can deal a mortal blow."

The things we don't know can kill us.

The trouble is, business owners are asked every day to step into the unknown. Business is fraught with far-reaching decisions that must be made before we have enough wisdom or experience or data to understand the full impact of our choices.

Sometimes all we can do is make a leap of faith.

Everything about owning a business is risky. Starting a business is a risk. Growth is a risk. Selling or merging or expanding—all are risks. Every decision and every move become risky when the neck that's on the line is ours. Can we afford to hire that key player? Can we afford to upgrade our technology? Can we afford not to? Not taking those risks can be the biggest risk of all. A business driven by fear will stagnate. And a stagnant business will die.

We can't be business owners without dealing with the risks. Take enough risks and you're bound to lose a bet here and there.

And what we risk when we lose a bet is always significant. We risk revenue. We risk the livelihood of people who depend on us. We risk the kids' college fund. We risk our freedom and our pride. Often, we risk our homes. The stakes are high, all the money on the table is ours and nobody wins every hand.

So we make assumptions. We rely on the lessons of past experience. We line up our actions against what we believe to be true. If we're smart, we ask questions and listen to the answers. We get advice. But most often we trust our gut because our instincts have typically served us well.

Entrepreneurs have the reputation for being risk takers. In reality, with so much at stake, we're pretty risk averse. So we learn to minimize the risks. We learn to hedge our bets.

Lifeblood Plus
Let's Assume These Are the Laws of Hedging

- The owner with the fewest assumptions and the most facts wins.

- Bad contracts are cement shoes that will take you down.

- Decide whether you can live with the worst case scenario.

- Every player is a bet.

- Firewall your family finances.

AVOIDING THE MORTAL WOUND

A dozen or so years ago, a woman launched a retail venture by renting booth space to diverse vendors with compatible and related wares. Her assumption was that buyers would be attracted to an atmosphere where they could engage in the same kind of thrill-of-the-hunt that attracts die-hard antiquers.

That assumption proved to be true.

A few years later, exhilarated by her success and looking to diversify her portfolio, she decided to buy a clothing boutique. She assumed that because she had succeeded in her first retail venture that she could transfer what she'd learned to operating this boutique.

That assumption proved to be wrong.

The customer base was different, the product was different, the venue itself was different. The basic formula that had worked in the original enterprise didn't transfer to the new store.

The price tag for this faulty premise ran into seven figures. Ten years later, when I first met her, her once robustly profitable business was still saddled with $750,000 in debt, pushing it dangerously close to the edge of failure.

That young woman didn't understand that unsupported guesswork can deal a mortal blow. ***Never underestimate the dangers of a false assumption.***

Hedging a bet is the art of minimizing exposure while our assumptions are being tested.

In a world where confidence is a prerequisite, false assumptions thrive. We get confident of our judgment and pretty soon we forget we aren't dealing with facts. Somebody said it, so we believe it. Common knowledge becomes solid business intelligence. Estimates become data. Conviction becomes wise counsel. Then we start basing our judgments on information that isn't accurate. A false assumption is born.

Acting on one major false assumption can take a business under— or come close, especially when the price tag for a false assumption can be in the millions. Even a smaller theory that proves to be wrong can have a big impact on the lifeblood of a business.

Here's another example of a simple, understandable false assumption that came with a $50,000 price tag.

Some years ago, the trade show marketing company I had bought as a turnaround had a significant opportunity when one of our national clients wanted a custom exhibit for a major trade show exhibit in Chicago —a big-time venue where the floor marshal Gestapo maintain a highly regulated environment. I felt confident that I was on solid ground because I'd put together a team of top-notch craftsmen; their background was in building store fixtures, but I made what I thought was a safe assumption: their skills would transfer to the trade show marketing arena. So I showed up on the trade show floor confident that the installation would go smoothly.

Sadly, my assumption that my production crew had the necessary controls and systems in place to meet the requirements of the customer and the exhibit hall proved to be wrong. Our customer's exhibit was two inches—that's right, *inches*—too tall—that's right, too *tall*; it wasn't even encroaching on anyone else's territory. Reason said two inches in a 2.2 millon-square foot exhibit hall was insignificant. Fire code and show marshals, however, said this high-dollar, custom exhibit had to come down...two inches.

We disassembled the entire exhibit and trimmed two inches off the top.

That false assumption cost my company $50,000 at a time when we were already fighting to survive on our existing lifeblood. I don't even want to think about what it cost in reputation and customer confidence.

An assumption is nothing more than our best guess about what will happen if we take a certain action: If we hire the heavy hitter, sales will go up. Or: If we raise prices, revenue will go up. Or maybe: If we raise prices, customers will go away. Even: If we move to a bigger facility, productivity will go up or we'll attract a caliber of clientele willing to pay more for our services because we've impressed them with our image.

When we hedge our bets, we're simply taking measures to avoid delivering a mortal wound to the lifeblood of our company if our assumptions turn out to be wrong.

THE BIG THREE GAMBLES

Wealth Builders hedge their bets in three key areas of business: people, growth moves and contracted agreements.

People: One of the biggest points of pain for any business is bad personnel moves. Nowhere else in the business do we make more false assumptions. We assume people will be honest, loyal, capable of everything we hired them for. We're blindsided when our golden boy sales rep leaves and takes his relationships with him. We're stunned when a key leader is building a business within our business, spawning competition on our time and our money. Hiring the wrong person, hanging onto the wrong person and trusting the wrong person all cost money and cause disruption.

The safe assumption: Every player is a bet.

Growth moves: Prepare for growth, but don't lunge. It's easier to get poor quick than it is to get rich quick. One big growth move is riskier than a series of small moves, so hedge your bets by planning for growth in stages. Here's an example. Many of my business owner clients want to expand their company's geographic footprint. Some want to go national—or today, international. Others just want regional presence. Smart ways to make those moves include following a customer who is expanding, giving ourselves a built-in client base; acquiring a smaller operation in the location you want, which avoids the costs and uncertainties of a start-up elsewhere; systematizing and codifying what you do so you can franchise it when the right player in the right location shows up. In every case, risk has been minimized, the cost of failure lowered.

The safe assumption: Use facts to grow familiar with the unknown.

> ## Owners Speak
>
> *"When people come to me and want to be part of my company, I say, 'Are you are willing to work for $500 a week until you learn the business?' I don't care how much experience they've got in the restaurant business, I'm not going to take a chance on them."*
>
> **George Couchell, Founder and Owner**
> **Showmars Restaurants**
> **Founded 1982; 800 full-time employees**

Contracts: A bad contract is like a pair of cement shoes, dragging us down when we get into deep water. Yet we sign them all the time, as we must. Leases, purchase agreements, agreements with customers and vendors. I'm certainly not advocating a commitment-less business environment. In fact, a good written agreement becomes the basis for trust in our business partnerships. But we're prone to go to contract before we know what our assumptions are and what the consequences will be if our assumptions are wrong. Sign on the dotted line only when you can live with the worst case scenario outcome. Try to make sure every contract has a back door that you can afford to exit.

The safe assumption: The business owner with the fewest assumptions wins.

Forecasting false assumptions

Unless we're going to be paralyzed by inaction, we must weigh our assumptions every day. The bigger the decision, the greater the impact of a false assumption on the lifeblood of the business. Ironically, a business practice we all rely on is nothing but applying assumptions to the lifeblood of the business: forecasting.

If assumptions are so dangerous, how do we avoid those dangers when we're forecasting our numbers for the months ahead as part of our strategic decision-making process? Forecasting as a disciplined process gives us information against which to measure our assumptions; it also demonstrates how to test other assumptions. We can follow these steps to minimize the assumptions made when forecasting our numbers:

1. Look back before we look forward. Pull as much specific historical data as possible on company financials. Break the numbers down monthly or quarterly; break them down by profit center. The more precise our numbers, the more accurate our projections.

2. Identify our assumptions. And understand that they are assumptions, not facts. When we see consistent patterns of monthly, quarterly or seasonal activity, we have to guard against locking in on one assumption before we've explored all the possibilities. No matter how strong our gut feeling, we must safely assume that we're dealing with at least one false assumption.

3. Separate facts from fiction. Be prudent in estimating what kind of revenue we can count on each month through contractual relationships or customer retention. Factor in every monthly expense. Err on the side of caution. Business owners are optimistic and it's easy to be overly optimistic.

4. Project the numbers. Based on sales history, what is a reasonable expectation for new monthly revenue? What is a likely rate of growth based on history as well as present sales and marketing efforts? What costs will go up this year, including growth-related costs (materials, staffing, equipment, facilities, etc.)? Pull it all together in a pro forma that communicates **what must happen** each month to achieve company goals.

5. Review results. Systematically examine our assumptions against reality. The flash report is a down-and-dirty weekly or bi-weekly reality check. Take a close look once a month. Take a hard look every 90 days. When our business is in a high risk period, we can step up our timeframe for review. This will allow us to identify our false assumptions earlier. And at each monthly and quarterly review, make sure everybody knows how close we come to the mark.

And always remember, assumptions aren't facts and neither are forecasts.

TESTING OUR ASSUMPTIONS

False assumptions can kill us. But every day in the life of a business owner requires sifting through assumptions to get to the facts and make decisions. We can't avoid assumptions because we can't avoid making decisions.

The best we can do is hedge our bets by minimizing our exposure while we test our assumptions.

Here's an example with a happy ending. Some years ago I had the opportunity to buy a business. It wasn't healthy, not by a long shot, but I made some carefully considered assumptions.

- Assumption 1: I believed I could turn it around and make it profitable.
- Assumption 2: I believed I could redefine the business.
- Assumption 3: I believed I could implement a better sales strategy.
- Assumption 4: I believed the brand was strong enough that I could capitalize on it.
- Assumption 5: I believed I could improve the sales cycle.
- Assumption 6: And I believed I could build a successful leadership team.

That's a lot of assumptions. A lot of room for the one false assumption that would mean losing my shirt. With that many assumptions, I knew I needed to seriously limit my exposure, my potential for loss.

First, I had to limit the money I invested.

Second, I had to give myself a back door so I wouldn't lose everything I had invested.

Third, I wanted the option to walk away with no penalties except my own lost time and (limited) investment capital.

I couldn't eliminate all the risks, but I could narrow my assumption base and shift as much risk as possible to the seller.

Here's how it played out. The deal was structured as an option to buy, with a short and specific buy-out date and an agreed-upon price. I put $15,000 on the table, with the understanding that I would pony up another $750,000 if I exercised my right to buy. And I insisted on complete ownership authority while I tried to turn the business around.

I proved my assumptions. When the option period ended, I paid for the business with the retained earnings I had accrued while turning the company around.

If my assumptions had been wrong, the worst-case scenario is that I could have walked away with invaluable experience and out $15,000. However, in this case, eight years later, I sold that company for $3.2 million, netting $1 million in profit.

Hedging our bets won't always net us $1 million in profit. Let me hedge my bets here and say there may even be a day when it won't save us from losing our shirts. But hedging our bets will minimize the times when we need to say, "If I knew then what I know now..." It happens to everyone, but business owners can't afford the luxury of too many false assumptions, any more than they can afford the luxury of waiting until every solution is clear.

The Smart Money guys have mastered the art of narrowing their assumptions by testing them. Every assumption they prove or disprove becomes experience which they can leverage to make decisions based

Lifeblood Plus
Trust Your Gut and Back It Up with Numbers

Many of us hate forecasting. We'd rather rely on our gut. Our industry is too unpredictable. We don't want to get locked into anything. Some of us are just afraid of saying it and then failing to achieve it.

Wealth Builders trust their gut because they've backed it up with numbers. Wealth Builders tame the unpredictability of their industry by studying previous years for patterns. Wealth Builders can afford to be flexible because they've planned for change.

Then there's that fear of failure. It's true, we may not always hit the numbers we project. But in the process of arriving at those numbers and expressing them to our team, we've given our business a head start on success.

on assumptions with less risk. Hedging our bets by leveraging our experience is as close as we can get to a sure-thing.

Ownership Perspective

1. Have you ever experienced an "arrogant moment" when your ego caused you to leap before you checked your assumptions?

2. Where must you constantly check assumptions before making decisions that will impact the lifeblood of your business?

3. Do you know good hedging when you see it? Who do you know in your life who has mastered this Hedging Your Bet rule?

SMART MONEY RULE #6
Leverage Down:

Under the surface of every business is untapped gold waiting to be mined.

CHAPTER NINE

SMART MONEY RULE #6:
LEVERAGE DOWN

"Smart Money never fails, it just evolves."

When it's broken, I don't want to fix it. I want to reinvent it. Innovate. Come up with a better idea to replace the one that isn't yet working perfectly.

Sometimes, that sparks an exciting new chapter in the life of my business. Sometimes it means the business spends hard-earned money on valuable assets that sit idle and under-utilized because I've decided to spend more money to accomplish something we already have the tools to accomplish.

It's part of my nature. In fact, that tendency to leap from one hot idea to the next is part of the entrepreneurial nature I see in almost every business owner. Most of us are visionaries; we love to create. But few of us have the patience to refine. Except for the rare breed of entrepreneur who delights in the painstaking process of seeking perfection in the details, it's against our nature to repeat and repeat until we get it right.

Innovation is on our DNA strand, right there with our survival instinct. We never want to be free of it, but we can't let it undermine execution. And we can't let it blind us to opportunities to increase the value of our business asset at the same time we preserve the lifeblood of the enterprise.

Wealth Builders have learned what our prudent mothers tried to tell us years ago: Make the most of what you've been given.

Sometimes we don't need to innovate; we need to go deep to mine the gold in our organizations. We need to leverage down.

SEEING POSSIBILITIES

One of my partners is the queen of making the most of what you have. When she bought her last home, she spent Saturday mornings looking for other people's cast-offs that she could turn into treasures

---

Lifeblood Plus
Leveraging experience

Answer these questions to find out whether you leverage the assets of experience and wisdom.

1) Do you have a board of outside advisors whose experience and objectivity you can leverage?

2) Do you have an identifiable process for evaluating company and individual mistakes in order to learn from them?

3) Do people in your company feel the need to cover up mistakes to avoid blame?

4) Which question does your company ask: *Whose fault is this?* Or *How did this happen and what can we learn from it?*

---

that mirror her personality and her wide-ranging passions. Her home is full of unexpected surprises.

On a wall in her home office she's hung a bright red-and-gold, metal six-foot by three-foot, molded tin Dr. Pepper sign. It looks as good today as it did when some Midwestern grocer hung it on the side of his building in 1949. She bought it for twelve dollars at a junk store in Nebraska 25 years ago and today collectors make her offers only she could refuse.

Her bookcases are filled with fifty-year-old hardcover classics scavenged from library reject sales—some of them still have their Dewey decimal system numbers marked on the spine. One is an illustrated first-edition Edgar Rice Burroughs.

She created a focal point in one area of her courtyard garden from the gravel and scraps of rock leftover when she finished her pond. She rooted an antique rose, mostly because the experts said it couldn't be done. It looked like a pitiful little stick with thorns for months; now its branches sprawl three feet in all directions. And every one of them is loaded with roses.

My partner sees possibilities.

She's the same with our work. When I say, *why don't we...*, she'll say, *Sam, we already did that.*

But I want to create it all over again, in new-and-improved form.

She says let's just improve on what we have.

In other words, leverage the assets you already have before you hunt down new ones. Leveraging the gold you have is always cheaper than mining for new gold. And the old vein is usually richer than the new vein.

SOFT ASSETS, HARD MONEY

Leveraging existing assets isn't as much fun as nailing the next big account or gearing up for the new product that's going to knock everyone's socks off. Leveraging isn't sexy. It doesn't get the adrenaline flowing. It doesn't give us the same satisfaction as watching our leaders scrambling to catch up with us before we come up with the next great idea. No, leveraging our existing assets is not shoot-the-rapids exhilarating.

It's just smart.

Most of us have more assets to leverage than we realize, and we're under-utilizing most of them because we fail to recognize them as assets. Capital equipment? Asset. Product inventory? Asset. Office furnishings? Asset. Intellectual capital? Put that one in the assets column, too.

Let's take a quick inventory of the assets we tend to overlook, assets that don't show up on the P&L, and see if we can't relate them to money in more tangible ways. Most of the assets we under-utilize will fall into two broad categories: talent and wisdom.

Talent. The typical business spends more money on people than almost any other asset. Yet it isn't putting this talent to its highest and best use. Is the best brain for building systems and procedures screwing up payroll every week because that employee is the easy solution, even

Lifeblood Plus
Snuffing Out Great Ideas

The most valuable wisdom we waste is our intellectual capital, the thinking power of our companies. Intellectual capital is everyone's best thinking, synthesized into a body of practices and knowledge for the purpose of illuminating, communicating and performing within the unique DNA of an organization.

Every time we disregard input from our leaders or hand them the solution to a problem instead of giving them an opportunity to solve problems, we're throwing away the thinking power, the experience, the collective creativity of the entire team. We're replacing it with our thinking alone. And while owners like to believe our ideas are worth ten of everybody else's, acting that way ultimately snuffs out the experience and creativity of others.

though the person is lousy with the books? It's very common to find a company's best sales person overseeing the sales team instead of closing prospects.

It even happens with owners. Some of us are managing people inside the company or overseeing production when we ought to be setting strategy or nurturing key account relationships. Delegation is the greatest tool we have for multiplying our capacity as owners. Yet we squander our greatest talents because we don't teach others how to do what we do. We hang onto the small stuff long past the point when we should've passed it down the line.

In recent years, I've worked with three different owners who were so buried in the work of the business they couldn't get to the work they were uniquely gifted to do.

The first owner drove trucks because he believed he couldn't afford to hire enough drivers to keep the trucks rolling. Of course he couldn't afford drivers. He was the number one sales guy, and he was *driving a truck*! Not only did this make it nearly impossible for him to hunt opportunities, when an opportunity did show up, he missed it because he was too busy shifting gears.

The second owner relished her role as the deal maker. Put her in front of a prospect and she could close the deal. It wasn't unusual for her to have a $10 million deal in her pocket. But the business wasn't prepared to capitalize on the opportunity because it didn't have a CEO. This owner had never raised up a leader who could manage the day-to-day operations; she was paying for the talent, she just wasn't applying it well. When she was playing in the minors, she could handle the two key positions of CEO and key account salesperson. But when the game began to heat up, nobody was warming up in the bullpen to take over the day-to-day for her.

Owner number three enjoyed the adrenaline rush of his company's rapid-response disaster restoration and repair service so much that he almost missed the chance to franchise his operation when the time was right. He allowed the entire organization to be driven by the unpredictability of fires, floods and weather-related disasters—everyone was expected to slide down the pole when the fire bell rang. The company could gain no momentum to build the infrastructure and disciplines that franchising would require because all the talent was pulled into crisis and chaos.

Lifeblood Plus
Seek Wise Counsel

We can all benefit from a fresh perspective and the wisdom others gained the hard way. But few of us bring together our trusted advisors to aid us in making difficult and crucial decisions. Most of us have an attorney, an accountant, maybe a financial planner, but their input is typically fragmented and tactical, not part of an integrated strategy. If you don't have an advisory board, create one.

When that owner pulled himself out of the fray and became the enterprise architect, his opportunity to franchise took root. He began to leverage the success of his business model through a franchising strategy that duplicates his success one business unit at a time. Today, he's on his way to building business wealth.

Leveraging is not a soft concept. These three owners were paying dearly—in hard dollars and lost opportunities—for the failure to leverage their talent.

If we evaluate every key player on our team, whose talent are we wasting because it's expedient or because we feel we don't have another option? And what are we losing when we do so? A player's rich network of contacts? Insights into operational efficiencies? Someone's unique ability to motivate and bring out the best in others? Ultimately, will we lose these players and every penny and every hour we've invested in them because they left for positions that allowed them to work out of their sweet spot?

Here's what's working at my company. Every key player is riveted on the one thing he or she is best gifted to contribute to the company. Our managing partner is no longer bogged down in nuts-and-bolts consulting; he's been elevated to high-level interventions, investment banking projects and leading in strategic planning for consulting clients. We have a player whose strength is a systematic, logical approach to problem solving, making him the obvious choice for leading in enterprise architecture. We have a CFO whose sole focus is monitoring results against a client's financial goals. And we have a player whose greatest talent is patience—that's my assistant.

And now that we're all highly focused on the things we do best, the business is executing better than it ever has. I'm leveraging the talent in my company.

What are you doing to leverage the talent you're paying for?

Wisdom. Failing to leverage knowledge, experience, lessons learned should be a capital offense for business owners. Guilty, your honor, of squandering in the first degree, punishable by a slow, painful death.

Every mistake, every failure, every experience, decision and initiative has an ROI—it comes when we evaluate what's happened and apply what we just learned to the next venture. Smart Money never fails, it just evolves. Wealth Builders don't look at mistakes like money out of their wallet. Instead, every experience—from miserable failure to unprecedented success—is simply a lesson for which a price was paid. The only real mistake is failing to mine the lessons in order to get closer to success, or to elevate the level of success.

One of the most damaging ways we fail to leverage wisdom and experience is in creating a culture of blame. As the owner we determine whether our companies look for a scapegoat or look for a lesson. When our companies are focused on laying blame, people will cover up their mistakes, making it impossible to improve or avoid those same mistakes in the future. We can keep paying the price for mistakes again and again, or we can get the pay-off for mistakes by using them to drive continuous improvement.

TAKING STOCK

In my work with business owners, we encourage three levels of leveraging the collective wisdom of the organization. Level one is a process to continuously improve execution at 90-day intervals. Level two allows the organization to harvest the gold of an entire year before the greatest successes and the most significant lessons are forgotten. Level three is our personal reflection on our role as owner.

Level 1: The 90-day review. My company has leveraged its experience in building businesses to create an Enterprise Architecture process. The process is driven by a closed-loop system for excellent execution and continuous improvement.

Every 90 days, company leaders evaluate performance against a measurable plan to see what's working and what's not. Based on the review, plans are improved and refined. Better strategies are employed.

Lifeblood Plus
The Annual Retreat –
Get Honest, Get Focused, Get Fired Up

The most important thing to remember about planning your company's annual retreat is to avoid a what-the-boss-wants event, where people's eyes glaze over and they laugh at all the right moments. What you want is a thinking event, where people get honest, get focused and get fired up.

Here are the steps to make that happen.

Timing is everything. A new calendar year traditionally marks a time for change, renewal and recommitment. Many companies begin a season of reflection late in the fourth quarter of the year or the first month of the new year.

Set the stage. A week ahead of time, make sure the leaders who will attend have: 1) a copy of last year's written strategic plan, the business plan or other strategic documents that capture where the company thought it was headed when the current year began; 2) probing questions to provoke fresh thinking.

Resources may be re-allocated. Faulty assumptions are spotted before they become major crises.

Ninety days at a time, the company improves its strategic thinking and its execution by taking an account of its progress. This simple process is the most effective way to leverage our company's experience.

Level 2: The annual retreat. The most successful businesses make time at the end of each year to step back and mine the golden nuggets from the year just ending. This becomes the natural first step in planning the year ahead. The best way to do this is at an annual retreat for company ownership and leadership.

We use two tools at our annual retreats that allow companies to gain greater clarity about how the business stands today compared to one year ago. Some companies use our Business Asset Profile year after year, watching the evolution in key areas like sales, marketing, communication, trust, use of resources and more. The Business Unit

---

Reflect. Owners and leaders tend to rivet their thinking on tactics and action. When we do, we compromise thinking power. So don't just jump into solutions. Make the first session of your retreat a time to reflect on the highlights of the year just ending.

Ask driving questions. Remember those probing questions distributed the week before the retreat? After reflection, it's time to answer them. What can we do to win the game? What stands in our way? What are the critical functions we must master to win the game? How will the business be different when we do? What will it mean in terms of new roles, new systems, new structure? This is where "we've always done it that way" thinking transforms into innovation and a "that's your problem" mentality shifts to collective problem-solving.

Map out the future. Set reasonable projections for the year ahead and come up with a plan to hit them. Prioritize goals and agree on the best leader for each goal, project or initiative. Write down the plan for the next 90 days and sketch out the three 90-day periods after that.

Scorecard provides a measurement of execution, customer relations, innovation and other critical success factors for profit centers of the business. Most companies love the graphs that give tangible proof of their progress from year to year. But what owners love is the enthusiasm and motivation of their leaders when they can track the effects of their work.

In fact, the discipline of an end-of-year retreat can become a defining moment for the business, empowering its leaders and shifting its focus in ways that are profound and positive. When companies leave our end-of-year mountaintop retreats, they launch into the new year with heightened awareness of how to avoid yesterday's mistakes and create tomorrow's successes.

Level 3: Ownership inventory. Our role as owner offers the chance to take stock in unique ways. As the year ends, I like to reflect on my vision for the company. I evaluate how well company directions are aligned with that vision. I determine what I could do more of—and less of—to make progress toward my vision. Setting goals in each area of life—physical, relational, spiritual, mental and professional—greatly increases the probability that I'll actually make the changes I desire.

VALUE OF A GOOD MISTAKE

Every three years, a business transforms itself. That's not a suggestion, it's a fact. We'll be better or worse, but we'll never remain the same.

The purpose of leveraging our experience is to make certain the business is transforming according to our plan and our vision, not randomly or reactively.

Thomas Watson—not the IBM guy, but the 17th-century theologian who became embroiled in the tug of war between the Anglican and Catholic churches—once said, "If you want to increase the speed of your success, you must increase the rate of your failure."

Mistakes create learning opportunities. Learning leads to excellence and excellence always gives a shot in the arm to the lifeblood of the business. Will you capture the capital of your mistakes? Smart Wealth Builders know the value of a good mistake.

Ownership Perspective

1. Do you treat intellectual, human and time capital as if it is as valuable as money?

2. In what ways might your drive to create become a hindrance to achieving excellence in execution?

3. Make a list of all the soft assets of your business. Which ones are under-leveraged?

4. What is your natural reaction to mistakes and misfires? What effect does your reaction have on the thinking power of those under your employ?

SMART MONEY RULE #7
Think Like a Capitalist:

Prepare for the day when an infusion of capital can elevate the wealth-building potential of the business.

Chapter Ten

Smart Money Rule #7:
Think Like a Capitalist

"The ultimate price of having no capital plan could be that there is no end in sight to your time on the ownership treadmill."

If your instincts told you it was time for your next big move, do you know where the capital would come from?

You know what I mean. Your radar tells you it's time for expansion or equipment or acquisition—the next natural step in maturing your enterprise. It won't come cheap, but it's time. How will you pay for it?

Maybe your capital plan works like this: *I'll figure it out.* Or, *I'll work my tail off and scrape together enough money to bootstrap it—again.*

Some of us leave to chance our big-picture strategy for the capital needs of our business. Or we think we can carry it on our own backs long enough for the business to start clicking. We think if working hard isn't working, we'll just work harder. We'll make any kind of personal sacrifice to keep the doors open—except showing forethought to the financial needs of a growing business.

Here's a three-step evaluation of your present level of capital planning.

1. Have you consciously identified strong candidates as sources you can tap for capital when the company needs more than you can fund on your own?
2. Are you deliberately cultivating those sources now?
3. Will you recognize the moment in the life of your business when the equity value of the company could make a significant leap with the right capital funding?

Let's say the answer to those questions is "no."

No, you don't have a capital plan, but with enough shoulder to the wheel, the money will take care of itself.

Or, no, you don't have a capital plan, but have the belief that if you can't manage it on your own cash flow or within your personal assets, it isn't worth the control you'd have to trade off?

The first belief—with hard work the money will take care of itself—is reckless denial. The 99% perspiration theory of success sounds good. But don't let all that sweat pouring off your forehead blind you to the

---

Lifeblood Plus
Debunking the Growth Myth

Most business owners I know cherish the myth that growth will solve all their money problems. Who needs a capitalist? We'll just sell more. Get more customers. Make an acquisition. Crank up the volume and our problems will be solved.

In reality, the cost of growth is always more than we ever estimate. And the returns are always slower coming in than we ever estimate.

Few businesses will survive significant growth without a source of outside capital. A good rule of thumb from the Smart Money guys is to have that money lined up no matter how confident you are that the money machine is now at full throttle.

---

need for a transfusion of capital to keep the lifeblood of the business flowing. Don't get caught by the Pollyanna principle that somehow the money will always show up.

The second belief—using outside capital isn't worth trading off control—is a value choice that is yours to make, as long as you realize the trade-off: limiting the potential of your enterprise by taking all the risk on your shoulders. When the need for money rears its head, the owner who is resistant to outside capital often falls into reactive decision-making and a short-sighted fear of loss.

PRIDE BEFORE THE FALL

Sara brought my company in to prepare her technology firm for sale and to represent her in the transaction. What we discovered when we went in to evaluate this business was that, even in a growth industry, this owner would have trouble getting the asking price she had in mind.

This company had been throttled by the owner's scarcity mentality for so long that it had damaged the value of the asset. The owner thought she could cost-cut her way out of her money problems. Sara took the legs off the business and still expected it to accelerate its way out of the cash shortage.

> **Lifeblood Plus**
>
> Capital *partners* aren't a prerequisite for business wealth. Capital *planning* is.

This owner's decision to capitalize everything herself put the business through an extended cash shortage that affected the company's ability to grow even after the cash shortage was over.

A number of things had happened as a result of the owner's ingrained pride in her ability to handle it all herself. First, scarcity of resources to improve or even do its best had lowered the bar on quality. The company mentality was to squeeze every dollar, even if it meant cutting corners in materials or ability to deliver excellent service.

Also, everyone in the organization had been exhausted by four years of simply trying to survive. They weren't at their best; in fact, some of the best had finally jumped ship because ownership couldn't—or wouldn't—compensate them at market rates. The ones who remained felt used up. They wouldn't create a favorable impression with would-be buyers.

Lifeblood Plus
Is it Time?

What are the telltale signs that a business needs an infusion of outside capital in order to move the business to its next life stage?

- You're dangerously close to failing to meet payroll more than once in any given quarter.

- You feel like the world is on your shoulders.

- Your net worth is threatened every payroll.

- You turn away from growth opportunities because you can't fund them.

The third consequence of Sara's decision to move through times of scarcity on her own was perhaps the most damaging one of all—and a cost most owners would never know or understand.

The people in this company lost their belief in the business. The strain of inadequate working capital reversed their trust. It robbed them of their hope.

Sara is a typical entrepreneur. Most of us take pride in being able to do it without help. We don't need help and we don't want interference. So we struggle. Sometimes we miss opportunities and bottleneck growth. Like Sara, we may discover that the spirit of our organization has been broken. Opportunities pass us by. The company's value as a marketable asset takes a dive.

That's what we can create when we operate our enterprises on the all-American myth that we can do it all ourselves.

FEAR AND LOATHING

Another myth has us running from anything with the smell of outside investment about it. A mythological demon I call the Vulture Capitalist has us by the throat.

Some of us make it one of our primary goals to elude the clutches of the Vulture Capitalists, the last-resort guys who are there for the up-against-the-wall entrepreneur who's been turned down by the rest of the world. Our fear and loathing of this mythical capitalist drives us to shoulder an impossible burden. Some of us, in the end, resist the notion of outside capital for so long that healthy strategic investors won't take a look at our cash-starved companies.

These are business owners who easily end up at the mercy of Vulture Capitalists, who swoop down right before the business dies and grab it up for next to nothing.

Moving beyond all these mental roadblocks against outside capital requires shifting our beliefs and attitudes about capitalists.

Lifeblood Plus
Benefits of a Capital Plan

- You share the burden.

- You can multiply wealth.

- You're motivated to succeed.

- You're empowered to get more of what you want out of business ownership.

The Wealth Builder learns how to identify the right kinds of capitalists and how to tap those sources in ways that are shrewd and low-risk.

But first, let's dissect the vulture.

The Vulture Capitalist does, indeed, scan the economic landscape looking for wounded prey. He's looking for: a) business owners who are operating out of the most fear; b) under-valued equity; c) owners who are over-aggressive and unrealistic about what's possible, even with an infusion of capital. His goal is to find an owner in the desert and offer him a glass of water—a very small glass of water that's priced with built-in penalties. Time then works against the optimistic owner who can't quite hit his marks, which then kicks in a higher rate of interest or return. The cash-starved business is buried by impossible obligations.

A Vulture Capitalist is smart and he has the upper hand from day one; he will eventually drag down even the most enthusiastic and determined entrepreneur.

Faulty—which is to say shortsighted, stubborn, maybe even a little ego-driven—beliefs about investment capital can kill our businesses.

Here are the truths the Wealth Builder lives by:

- Most highly successful enterprises reach a point when they need capital beyond the resources of ownership if they are to achieve significant equity value.
- The smart business owner plans for the day when the business will need more capital.
- The resulting capital plan empowers owners to achieve their wealth objectives.

The business owner who is unprepared exposes himself to investors who have earned the bad reputation sometimes associated with capital investors. If business owners were the subject of one of Aesop's fables—*The Vulture Capitalist and the Pigeon*, let's say—the moral would be simple: Either plan your capital strategy or learn to like the vultures.

Lifeblood Plus
Grim Fairy Tales

Three prevalent myths have grown up around the notion of outside capital.

1. All capitalists are predators.

2. Accepting outside capital is a sign of weakness.

3. Giving up equity means the owner has less.

These are *myths*. Don't fall for them.

A TALE OF TWO OWNERS

Listen to how different attitudes about outside capital impacted two business owners.

One was prepared to seize the moment and build an enterprise. The other one woke up one morning wondering what happened to the momentum. What made the difference? The answer lies in their attitudes about investment capital.

Eric is a classic one-gun slinger and a bootstrapper, proud to say he's done it all himself—no investment capital, no debt. One of his core beliefs is that hard work will pay off with top-line revenue. And he did work hard. The company became so healthy that expansion looked like a sure thing. Expansion would strain company resources, so Eric opened a line of credit on his house.

The expansion cost more than he'd budgeted. The returns weren't as high as he'd hoped. Eric realized he'd been overly optimistic. But all he needed was a little extra capital, just enough to buy time for this move to start paying off.

Eric's bank knew he was in pretty deep. Although he'd been a loyal customer for years, the bank wasn't willing to loan him the amount of capital he needed. That was no problem; there was a bank down the street that had been trying for years to get Eric's business. But Eric hadn't built relationships at that bank; his only contacts were sales bankers. Now that he needed this bank, the guys who controlled the purse strings saw a guy they didn't really know who was in over his head. If his own bank didn't have much confidence in him, why should they?

Owners Speak

"You have to decide whether you want to attack the market aggressively with somebody else's money or just have steady controlled growth."

Bob Confoy
HomeGuard Inc.
Founded 2003

Eric couldn't muster the capital he needed to take full advantage of the momentum he had worked so hard to build. The expansion never took off. The window of opportunity closed; he's stuck in the business and his house is on the line.

Then there's Katherine. Katherine's pretty much a one-gun slinger, too, like most entrepreneurs. She was determined to live inside her cash flow; she had a plan for making that work in the early years of the

---

Lifeblood Plus
Potential Results of No Plan

Suppose you don't have a capital plan. Here are some possible consequences:

- Things cost more than you expect and the returns aren't as high as you'd hoped.

- You need a little extra capital, but without planning, it's hard to get your hands on it.

- Organic growth is slower because resources are more limited.

- Momentum may be lost, which often means you miss opportunities.

- The control is all yours. So is the risk. You may miss opportunities because of lower risk tolerance.

- Some windows of opportunity may close permanently.

- The needs of a maturing business may not be fully met with limited resources.

The price of having no capital plan could be finding yourself on the cusp of significant expansion with no way to seize it. The price of those missed opportunities could be lost revenue. The price of lost revenue could be the risk of losing key players who can't defer forever and decide to look for greener pastures. The ultimate price of having no capital plan could be that there is no end in sight to your time on the treadmill.

Only you can weigh whether those trade-offs are worth the control you hang onto because your only capital plan was to dig deeper into your own pockets.

business. The plan, she knew, wouldn't be possible without stakeholders who believed in her: employees who believed in Katherine's vision and were willing to defer rewards in order to be a part of the venture; vendors who were willing to give her favorable terms; bankers she'd been working with for years who extended a little credit here and there.

Katherine even met a couple of people over the years who said they believed in her vision enough to invest in it. Katherine knew the needs of the business were still manageable within her cash flow, but she nevertheless cultivated those relationships, turning to them as advisors. So when she saw that she would soon need an infusion of

Lifeblood Plus
Potential Results of Capital Planning

Capital partners aren't for everyone. But what if you'd made the choice to devise a capital strategy that created the right kind of capital for the right moment in the life of your business? What might that look like?

- You have multiple capital options, including a number of banks and potential investors. With so many options, you're able to structure the best terms.

- Cash on hand and cash reserves are healthy.

- Early-stage employees begin to see the rewards, and their commitment deepens.

- You've established true market value and equity value for your company.

- If you chose investors as part of your capital plan, you now have additional stakeholders who are committed to helping you succeed.

- You've elevated your accountability for success to your stockholders, including yourself.

- The risk is no longer all on your shoulders.

- You ride the momentum to the next life stage of your business..

cash to fund an expansion, it was time for Katherine to harvest those relationships. While maintaining majority control and for a reasonable amount of equity, she gained not only the cash she needed, but two more stakeholders who had a vested interest in her success.

When Katherine received the capital from her investors, she went to her bankers and opened a line of credit as a hedge against the unexpected. She went down the street to the bank that had wanted her business for years. Based on the solid foundation of her cash on hand and her cash reserves, the new bank loaned her the money to make the growth move.

Lifeblood Plus
Power Shift

When a bank is soliciting a business owner, the owner has the power. When the owner attempts to go after the bank, the banker has the power. Take control of the power before that shift occurs.

Thanks to her investors, Katherine was able to make her move without touching the investment capital.

The story of Katherine's successful expansion didn't have a surprise ending. Katherine had planned it all along.

Two business owners, both freedom-minded entrepreneurs, both experiencing successful growth in a niche market. One is stuck on a treadmill. The other is launching to a new level of wealth.

The lesson in these two stories lies in the beliefs underlying their different responses to the same circumstances. One owner thinks a capital strategy is constructed for the needs of the day, or the moment. When you need it, see what you can get your hands on. The other owner sees a capital strategy as part of a plan to grow the business. This owner is practicing the Wealth Builder's principle of perspective: Always get ahead of your need for capital.

THE HUNT FOR OPPORTUNITIES

What exactly is a capital plan?

It is *not* knowing years in advance how much capital we'll need and marking it on the calendar so we don't miss the deadline. Business changes too fast and too frequently for that to be possible. Capital planning starts with staying attuned to the business and its needs, including calculations about what those needs will be in future stages of the business. Before the hawk in us begins to hunt opportunities for capital, we cultivate the eagle eye that sees the big picture of the enterprise's needs in the months and years ahead, long before the business is hungry for capital.

Step by step, here's what capital planning looks like.

1. Make the Big Decision. Owners with a capital plan have made the decision to place the needs of the business ahead of their own immediate needs. They realize they

are growing an asset with its own needs, its own lifestages of growth.

2. Leverage the vision. Vision helps owners identify future needs of the business at different stages. Ownership paints the picture of the company's growth so distinctly that it's possible to foresee the day when the business will need certain key employees, a facility with specific capabilities, advanced technology or upgraded equipment, a definable geographic footprint. That vision not only enables owners to keep the needs of the future clear in their own mind, it helps accomplish the next important step in capital planning.

3. Engage non-equity stakeholders. Early-stage stakeholders can provide invaluable capital resources at a time when financial resources are in short supply. These stakeholders might be employees who are passionate about the vision, bankers who see the possibilities and watch successes pile up, vendors who can support a young business with favorable terms, clients and customers who buy into a long-term relationship. Each of these strategic allies is staked into the game in some way because the vision has been cast in a way that is powerful and memorable.

4. Take the necessary steps to become investable. Most imperative of all is creating a systems-driven enterprise that does not require the owner's daily presence in order to be a profitable business asset.

5. Build strategic financial partnerships. Owners who think like capitalists don't wait until they need bankers or other financial sources

---

Lifeblood Plus
Different species of capitalists

Self-funders: Many early-stage entrepreneurs shoulder the whole burden. The idea of reaping all the rewards while controlling your own destiny has appeal. This is sometimes offset by a very real downside: The risk is high and yours alone. And the rewards may be limited or very long in coming because there is less capital to fund growth. What the self-funder wants: control.

Friends & family: This is one of the most common sources of investment capital, but one that offers big potential for entanglements. If you go this route, spell out all the conditions and expectations clearly and often. Make sure your investors know every dollar could be lost and how long it might be before they expect a return. For yourself, be very clear about any expectations that may come with the investment; some friends and family may feel their investment gives them say-so about how that money is used. Spell it out, for everyone's sake. What friends and family want: To not lose their shirts.

---

to build those relationships. This step becomes the basis for rainy-day funds and forms the base of credibility that makes financial sources willing to risk more capital with less secured collateral.

6. Cultivate capital sources. Smart Money owners cultivate relationships with potential capitalists who are interested in true partnerships so they can harvest those relationships when the time is right. The best relationships are cultivated for years before an investment is needed. These aren't Vulture Capitalists; they are the true investors who desire mutual success, not a chance to pick the bones.

7. Diversify fund sources. Create as many different avenues and options as possible for getting your hands on cash. Whenever possible, make sure the most accessible source is also the lowest-cost source of backup money.

8. Leverage investment capital. Look carefully at how Katherine used the capital she secured to create additional sources of capital before

---

Lenders: Commercial banks and other lenders are a type of capitalist who could play key roles at pivotal moments in your game. This is the best source of capital in town. What the lender wants: a sure-thing and the collateral to back it up.

Venture Capitalists: This isn't for everyone. But when you find yourself moving toward a golden opportunity that will need resources outside the comfort zone of traditional lenders, the right venture capitalist can be a true strategic partner and a key component in the Wealth Builder's capital plan. If that kind of opportunity fits your vision, it may be wise to cultivate these relationships long before the need arises. What venture capitalists want: significant reward in proportion with their risk and a specific plan for exiting the business with that reward proportionate to their risk; often, they also enjoy participation in the success of high-potential opportunities.

Vulture Capitalists: These are the last-resort guys who move in for the kill when companies have run out of options. What the vulture capitalist wants: to grab a dying business for next to nothing.

---

the initial investment was deployed in the business. She multiplied the capital and created elasticity in her capital resources.

A capital plan is the difference between the business owner who misses opportunities and the Wealth Builder who understands the strategic deployment of sufficient capital to grow through the healthy stages of development.

Are you protecting your enterprise with capital foresight?

CORE COMPETENCY

Developing a capital plan is a big leap from the simple starting point of learning to earn and keeping your eyes on the money. Every Smart Money Rule challenges business owners, no matter what the life stage of their business, to think differently about money and to treat it differently.

But capital planning is a notch above all the others. It is a rare animal who can take full advantage of the wealth-building potential of a business without mastering this core competency.

Be forewarned: capital planning is the precursor to a new realm of business ownership. Capital planning distinctly separates those who are satisfied with the results of playing by Smart Money Rules and those who seek the pathway to significant wealth. When you take this step, you are moving into territory that only a small percentage of business owners ever reach.

The territory of the Business Wealth Builder is ripe for conquering. Making the move requires commitment and courage, but I don't know a true entrepreneur who doesn't have both. And now you have the rules of the road.

Any business owner, any time, can answer the call.

Ownership Perspective

1. Have you ever experienced that gut wrenching moment of "no confidence" from your banker (who you thought was a trusted friend to your business)? How has that affected you today in the way you plan for the capital needs of your company?

2. Have you ever lost a significant wealth opportunity for your business because you did not have the capital on hand to seize the moment?

3. Is it difficult for you accept that you may need others to invest in your business for it to realize its fullest potential? And that to do so means that you create an asset that you share with others while, likely, making yourself wealthier?

THE WEALTH BUILDER'S CODE:

The Wealth Builder shifts success
measurements from revenue to earnings,
from earnings to equity,
from equity to portfolio wealth.

CHAPTER ELEVEN

DO YOU WANT TO BE RICH
OR DO YOU WANT TO BE WEALTHY?

*"We have enough money and enough freedom to pursue
whatever frontiers our spirit craves."*

Scouts for professional sports know when they've spotted a winner. They have a list of predictors—speed, strength, agility. They zero in on those predictors and watch athletes' games to see how they measure up.

Star quality in building a highly successful business is no different. There are traits and characteristics and practices that give a veteran enterprise scout a good feel for who can get it across the goal line.

But first, I guess, we all have to decide what we want our end game to look like.

Some of us might enjoy the scrimmage but want to stay out of the pressure cooker of a big game. Some of us might be thrilled with a league championship. But some of us...some of us just know that nothing less than the Super Bowl will do.

Top of the economic heap

I've never met a more unlikely Wealth Builder than Mike. In fact, almost anybody predicting Mike's future might've said he was more likely to end up in prison, a victim of violence or maybe just one of many missing-in-action fathers and husbands.

Mike could have been the poster child for disadvantaged youth. He's African American. He grew up in poverty. Fatherless, with a young mother. But he was smart and gifted and he saw a way out: professional sports.

We all know what a cliché that is: a kid growing up with nothing who thinks sports is his salvation. Those of us who are older and wiser know what a dead-end dream that is for the vast majority of young people. Instead of planning a realistic future of studying hard, staying out of trouble in spite of the odds and working their way up in an economic arena where the playing field is hardly level, they dream of playing ball. Hitting home runs and living large. Slam dunking their way to respect. Spiking the ball in the end zone and saying, "Look at me! I did it!"

The only odds any slimmer than a kid like that making it in professional sports are the odds of making it to the top of the economic heap. Here's how unrealistic Mike was: he planned to use professional sports to open the door to business ownership.

"I always knew I wanted to be a business owner," Mike said. "I could see myself walking into my board room in my suit, sitting at the head of the table."

Here's this enterprise scout's tip: put your money on Mike. I've been scouting Mike, looking at those predictors. He could make it to the Enterprise Super Bowl.

In 1997, Mike Minter signed with an NFL expansion team, the Carolina Panthers. On the field, Mike certainly measures up. He's one of today's most talented and respected players, not just for the Panthers, but throughout the NFL. He's certainly making all the money a kid who grew up in his circumstances could ever have dreamed of. What more could he want?

"I don't want to be rich," he says. "I want to be wealthy."

A few days before he left for football camp to prepare for the 2005 season, Mike and I met for an early-morning session in his library, before the kids were awake and before the rush to prepare for his departure started. But football wasn't at the top of his mind that day. At the top of his mind was his game of business.

Mike Minter could take all his marbles and just enjoy counting them. Instead, he has chosen to play smart with his money. He's invested in real estate development, a learning center, an upscale salon and spa with national-brand potential. He founded Recruits Unlimited, Inc., an Internet enterprise that gives high school athletes exposure to college coaches by making academic and athletic information and video footage available on-line. Mike's passion and his commitment to making these ventures successful is only step one in his long-range plan.

As I listened, the scout in me with the nose for Smart Money guys realized, "If this guy takes the time to learn how to build an enterprise and not just be an angel investor, he could be an enterprise star."

Here's what stood out about Mike. Yes, he wanted to make smart investments with the money he was earning—to get wealthy rather than just get rich. He also recognized that the kind of wealth he intended to build wouldn't come from putting his name on a franchise here and there or signing lucrative endorsement contracts. Mike's vision goes miles beyond that. He wanted his money to work for him. He wanted to build an enterprise empire that would secure his and his family's future while providing significant revenue for impacting the world. He had figured out that business is about more than the score; when scoring is all that matters, players miss a lot of what is happening on the field.

Mike had a vision few have when they found a business. He wanted to become the ultimate Wealth Builder.

RICH OR WEALTHY?

Are you satisfied just to be rich?

Or do you want to be like Mike: "I don't want to be rich. I want to be wealthy."

For some of us, learning to play by the Smart Money Rules will get us exactly where we want to be—rich. That means we're off the treadmill, or at least we've slowed it down to a manageable pace. We're not sweating bullets over payroll, although the big growth moves still give us a few knots in the stomach. We're even doing what we like doing best inside our business, most of the time. We feel like we've earned a degree of the freedom and autonomy we've always dreamed of.

Who could ask for anything more?

Another breed of entrepreneurs who gain financial health will still be hungry. Not so much hungry for more stuff, more toys, more privileges. But hungry for something beyond the level of success where the Smart Money Rules can take us. We're hungry for true wealth.

We want to build something significant. We want to see the summit beyond this summit, and conquer it, too. Remember our legacy? We're descended from pioneers, from bold adventurers who conquered a wilderness. People who still feel that spirit and answer the call of the Entrepreneurial Revolution won't be satisfied with 10 employees and $800,000 in revenue. As gratifying as that might be, *it just isn't enough*.

We're hungry for the ultimate challenge.

PRIVILEGES OF WEALTH

Those of us with the deepest well of pioneer spirit want to build wealth with our enterprises. Big wealth. We want to push ourselves beyond our limits.

We want something I call True Wealth.

And during our journey, we begin to realize that True Wealth is a realm beyond what we ever imagined.

Operating by Smart Money Rules opens the doors to a kingdom many of us never quite imagined. Sure, we expected—or at least dreamed—that playing smart at the game of business ownership could reap big tangible rewards. Some of us envisioned a house in a gated community or world travel or the ultimate car in the garage. Maybe we envisioned early, worry-free retirement. Or we might've envisioned giving our children opportunities we never had.

Wealth has its privileges, we've heard, and most of us who struggle long and hard to reach the summit won't turn down a few privileges. But it's also our nature to wonder, as we survey our success, "What next?"

Take a trip with me for a moment. Imagine that we've struggled to the summit of Great Enterprise. The journey wasn't easy. We slipped a few times, thought surely we were dropping off a cliff more than once. We sweated and wanted to stop and became convinced, sometimes, that we'd taken a wrong turn. At times, when we looked up at the peak we aspired to, we were given the second wind we needed to keep moving. Other times, the peak looked impossibly far away.

But we made it. Winded and a little worse for the wear, but we're here.

Now let's stand tall for a moment and savor the view from the top.

Heady stuff.

Maybe, for those of us who eat challenges for breakfast, a little anti-climactic?

Now imagine, as you take a 360 view, that you suddenly realize something you couldn't have known from the trails you've just conquered: looming above you in the distance is another peak.

Achieving Business Wealth makes available to us a realm of wealth we might never have considered.

A PECULIAR PLAGUE

Smart Money Rules provide us with the necessary tools to propel ourselves through the various stages of business ownership. They get us farther up the mountain.

But playing smart with our money is only the end game if we make that choice. Playing smart with our money actually expands the game, if we choose to keep moving up the mountain.

And most of us who make it that far will want to climb the next peak. Business ownership is a kind of progressive disease. Our spouses might even call it an addiction. Many of us call ourselves serial entrepreneurs.

Lifeblood Plus
The Four Stages of Business Ownership

Stage 1: Entrepreneur. We have an idea, find a way to finance it and reach an audience. The business is wrapped around us as we move through start-up and launch, astounding everyone when we reach the low six figures. We've found and inspired a few loyal people eager for the punishment of pulling the plow of a would-be enterprise. About all we have is a dream, but it's enough to keep us going when the bank statement looks pretty scary. The majority of businesses never make it past this point. We either go under or settle into a one-person shop existence that never makes us rich but still feels satisfying on some levels. We encounter a Smart Money Rule from time to time, but don't understand them well enough yet to follow them consistently. Success is measured by revenue.

Stage 2: Owner CEO. The business is taking shape, building systems and procedures and customer base. We run the show until the pace and the pressure make it impossible to do everything ourselves. A few leaders begin to grow up around us and gain our confidence and, in some cases, we begin to release responsibility into their hands. The business will break into seven figures, but how big the numbers get is in direct proportion to how willing we are to step back and give our leaders real authority. Time and again, we hit a ceiling of complexity and exhaustion that we break through only by handing off the reins to others. Some Smart Money owners stop here, unable or unwilling to move beyond this point. Success is measured by earnings.

The game may start small but few of us can stop there. The stages of our peculiar plague look like this:

1. Entrepreneur
2. CEO
3. Owner Capitalist
4. Enterprise Investor

Stage 3: Owner Capitalist. Leaders run the show. We've settled into a role that takes full advantage of our unique contribution to the business. We feel relief from stepping off the treadmill although the periodic crisis takes us back a step or two. Smart Money Rules are second nature to us and to our leaders, so revenue is consistently good, profit is reliable. Our leaders are reaping rewards, as well. Re-investing in the business has resulted in a valuable asset and our personal portfolio is healthy. Even so, we're developing more than one source of capital in case it's needed. But we're beginning to get restless. Our entrepreneurial spirit is getting tired of the status quo. Without wise counsel, we might buy a boat or stir things up and make moves just because we need a little adventure. This is when ill-considered acquisitions or expansions or other growth moves can cripple a thriving enterprise. Success is measured in equity value.

Stage 4: Enterprise Investor. The ultimate Business Wealth Builder, we've secured our finances both personally and inside the business. We saw this day coming and we've positioned ourselves to use a percentage of company profits as working capital outside the business. Our enterprise has become the ultimate wealth machine, where money begets money. We may or may not sell the original enterprise, but we steward our resources well. We satisfy our entrepreneurial spirit by supporting the growth of other young enterprises through angel investment and sometimes with our hard-earned wisdom. We can see countless new summits from where we stand and we are prepared to conquer them. We can select the challenges that are most meaningful to us. We have the best of all possible worlds: *We have enough money and enough freedom to pursue whatever frontiers our spirit craves.* Success is measured in portfolio wealth and in the intangibles I think of as True Wealth—family, faith, stewardship, peace of mind.

Those who don't understand the journey like to think that moving through these stages is a combination of luck and savvy, heavy on the luck. As I sit side by side with business owners, I see them making choices they don't even realize they're making. Our end journey is a by-product of our choices. When we understand the choices and make them consciously, we control our own destiny. It isn't just luck.

The journey from bold pioneer to True Wealth Builder requires a series of conscious choices. The choice to operate from Smart Money Rules can get us through stages one and two. The journey becomes more challenging, the choices more difficult as we elevate to the next stages. Every owner must make a conscious choice to continue the journey in order to move through the final two stages and arrive at True Wealth.

These shifts in perspective are the gradual result of the deliberate choice to operate by the Wealth Builder's Code.

Protecting, growing and retaining the lifeblood of the business— playing by Smart Money Rules—is point A in the Wealth Builder's Code. Without making this deliberate choice, entrepreneurs never become Wealth Builders. Sometimes we can make the Lifestyler choice and manage to maintain our status as entrepreneur and the illusion of independence. But at best, most Lifestylers are working for their business. At worst, they're working for the bank.

Successful navigation of this stage of the Wealth Builder's Code prepares us for the rest of the journey. We'll know we're ready for the journey when we can accept the challenges to:

1. Give up the cowboy routine and act like an owner. The owner is more than an executive leader, more than a manager, more than the big boss. At the top of every company is the one person who sets the tone for the organization by treating the business like a valuable asset. That person is the owner.

2. Face the inner enemies. If owners set the tone in their companies, they must face their enemies—even the ones that implicate them. They must become accountable for their entitlement mentality, their fears, the sacred cows that impact the entire organization and keep them from making wise choices that protect the business asset.

3. Put money in motion. Wealth Builders instinctively understand the concept of using the business as a platform to create cash for investments that put money into motion. Rule one of economic freedom: Don't work for your money; make your money work for you.

4. Pursue the extraordinary. Plenty of owners desire greatness; few have the gumption to go for it. When Mike Minter told me about sitting on the floor playing with his Lincoln logs as a little boy, not content to snap a few pieces together to make a simple house or car, I saw both the desire and the courage. Even as Mike was earning his degree in mechanical engineering at the University of Nebraska, he knew he was preparing himself for much more. When Wealth Builders have a dream, get out of the way.

5. Seek wise counsel. Entrepreneurs can think so expansively and so out-of-the-box that they're vulnerable to blowing things up. That's why it's invaluable to leverage the experience and insights of those who are farther along in their journeys.

Becoming the Business Wealth Builder requires choices that go beyond the actions we take with our money. Becoming the Wealth Builder affects the beliefs and values that underpin our use of money.

As we shift our success measurements from revenue to earnings, from earnings to equity, from equity to portfolio wealth, we also begin to make different choices about the very way we live our lives. We adopt the mind-set of the steward who neither hoards nor squanders, but puts his talents to work in service to a higher calling. We understand what it means to place our personal desires behind the needs of our enterprise, our family, our community. The high privilege of economic success brings with it another high privilege: the responsibility of becoming good stewards of all that we've been given.

SAM FROWINE

Wealth Builders are not the same driven-to-succeed one-gun slingers who started down the entrepreneurial pathway and stumbled into a revolution. Wealth Builders have built a legacy of prosperity and purpose for all those they touch. They expand the realm of True Wealth until it reaches far beyond the boundaries of a single enterprise.

Ownership Perspective

1. Do you clearly understand the difference between the views of the "rich" business owner versus the "wealthy" one? Which do you aspire to be?

2. If you have chosen the Wealth Builder journey, which stage are you in right now—Entrepreneur, CEO, Owner Capitalist or Enterprise Investor?

3. What will you have to give up in the way of habits and choices to embrace the challenge of becoming a true business Wealth Builder? If you intently engage in this True Wealth journey, what rewards can you expect?

CONCLUSION

Business ownership is a rich and risky game.

It is also a blessing and a trust for those of us who accept the challenge. It is our opportunity to respond to and rebuild economic and social systems that are breaking. It is our platform to make a difference in the world.

Business ownership opens the door to the realm of True Wealth.

One last story. It's a short one.

Tony Pope is one of the owners I've been privileged to walk with for many years. An entrepreneurial genius, he saw himself years ago in my description of the Lifestyler and decided he wanted something more for himself, his family and his business. Today, Tony engages every day in the challenging journey of the Wealth Builder. Like all of us, he doesn't get it right every day. But he sticks with the journey.

In the days after Hurricane Katrina devastated the Gulf Coast in 2005, I got a call from Tony. He said, "I'm filling up a truck and driving it down there. How much are you going to contribute?"

Moments like that humble me with the piercing truth of how much each of us contribute to the lives of others, how easy it is to make a difference, if we make the right choices.

Tony made a profound choice that each of us, as entrepreneurs, have the privilege to make.

Each of us plays the game in our own way. We get to choose our own playing field. We get to choose our own scoring criteria. We even get to make up our own rules, if that's the way we choose to play the game.

After all, that's why we're entrepreneurs, isn't it?

But no matter where you are in the game of your business, it's never too late to change your rules. As long as there's a dollar in the bank, it's never too late to start playing by Smart Money Rules. It's never too late to start reaping the benefits of following the Wealth Builder's Code.

The catch is that it isn't just about the money.

Money is the lifeblood, it's true. Mastering the practices that protect the lifeblood of our enterprise is a basic, a pre-requisite for success.

But mastering the game calls on us to radically redefine ourselves as business owners.

It calls on us to change our beliefs and values, to confront our fears, to dig deep for our true motives and purpose. It calls on us to change deeply and profoundly.

It's tempting to refuse the call. But once you've glimpsed the end game, it's hard to turn around and pretend you're satisfied with where you are today. You're at a crossroads.

Will you engage the journey?

APPENDIX

The Wealth Builder's Code

For more than a decade, Sam has been refining and integrating the best practices of highly successful business owners into a body of knowledge for business owners who desire to become Wealth Builders. This body of knowledge has become the Business Wealth Builder's Code. The Code is based on the hard-earned wisdom of experienced business owners who have contributed to the depth and breadth of the body of knowledge that makes up the Code.

I. Lifeblood is in the relationship between time and money: Healthy and rhythmic cash flow buys time to refine the success formula of the business.

II. The only person with the authority, the accountability and the unique perspective to build and cultivate the business as an asset with market value is the owner.

III. Every decision, every choice, impacts the lifeblood of the business.

IV. Making money is hard; hanging onto it is even harder.

V. Wealth Builders balance the need to survive the day with the importance of keeping an eye on the future.

VI. Business is a living organism; the lifeblood that sustains it must be protected.

VII. The vision of building a meaningful legacy unlocks the wealth potential of an enterprise.

VII. Owners cannot transform their businesses without transforming themselves.

VIII. Wealth Builders ingrain the principles of wealth building deep in the DNA of their organizations.

IX. Investing in the business creates equity appreciation; expenses are nonrecoverable and represent lost liquidity.

X. Business owners get rich by building rich relationships.

XI. The highest stage of enterprise building is converting company profits into a source of capital used to create a continuous stream of revenue independent of the entrepreneur's involvement.

The Language of the Wealth Builder

Sam developed the Wealth Builder's Code and the Enterprise Builder System over the course of more than two decades in the laboratory of ownership. Some of his language is unique to the practices and beliefs that make up the Code and the System.

Business Wealth Builder
The business owner who aspires to build a healthy enterprise that provides a source of sustainable income independent of ownership participation in the business of the business to attain sustainable income

Crossroads
Critical junctures in the life of business owners who are transitioning from their role in an owner-centered entrepreneurial pursuit to their new role in a leader-centered enterprise with financial sustainability

Entrepreneurial revolution
Dominance of successful private enterprise as the driving force behind economic health in the 21st-century

Grand Vision
Ownership's picture of how the business will look, feel and function when it has achieved a certain level of success that is linked to ownership's greater purpose for the enterprise

Great Enterprise
A sustainable wealth-generating machine that is legacy-bound

Image Lifestyler
A business owner whose primary purpose is to build a cash-generating machine that will support the desire for a particular lifestyle, typically tied to material comforts for ownership

Lifeblood

The resources of time and money that enable a business to sustain in order to refine and perfect its business model in order to cross the chasm and become a great enterprise

Quality of Lifestyler

A business owner whose primary purpose is to achieve a level of freedom to express individual talents via the business or to devote more time outside the business to family, hobbies or other personal interests

True Wealth

The state of mind and spirit that occurs when people use their talent and their passion to produce substantial financial return, while gaining deep satisfaction from work that is significant

Sam's Bookshelf

Wealth Builders learn, adapt and grow continuously. They are thinking people who remain open to new ideas and new perspectives. Reading allows business owners to tap the best thinking in the world as a way to improve their enterprise-building skills. These are a few of Sam's favorite reads, books that have had a powerful influence on the way he thinks and acts on his ownership journey. They're categorized here around four key concepts of Wealth Building.

Thinking Like a Wealth Builder

Allen, James, *As a Man Thinketh*. Barnes and Noble, Inc., early 1900s.

Brush, C.G.; N.M. Carter; E.J. Gatewood; P.G. Greene; M. Hart, *Insight Report, Women business owners and equity capital: The myths dispelled,* Kansas City, MO: Kauffman Center for Entrepreneurial Leadership, Marion Ewing Kauffman Foundation.

Brush, Candida; Nancy M. Carter; Elizabeth Gatewood; Patricia G. Greene; and Myra M. Hart, *Clearing the Hurdles: Women Building High-Growth Businesses*. Prentice-Hall, 2004.

Collins, Jim, *Good to Great: Why Some Companies Make the Leap… and Others Don't*. Harper Business, 2001.

Covey, Stephen R., *First Things First*. Simon and Schuster, 1995.

Crosson, Russ, *A Life Well Spent: The Eternal Rewards of Investing Yourself and Your Money in Your Family*. Ronald Blue and Company, LLC, 1994.

Csikszentmihalyi, Mihalyi, *Flow: The Psychology of Optimal Experience*. New York: Harper Collins Publishers, 1990.

Csikszentmihalyi, Mihaly, *Good Business: Leadership, Flow, and the Making of Meaning*. Viking, published by The Penguin Group, 2003.

Drucker, Peter, *The Age of Discontinuity: Guidelines for Our Changing Society*. Harper and Row, Publishers, 1968.

Fox, Jeffrey J., *How to Make Big Money in Your Own Small Business*. New York: Hyperion, 2004.

Frankl, Viktor, *Man's Search for Meaning: An Introduction to Logotherapy.* Boston: Beacon Press, 1959. 154.

Godin, Seth, *Purple Cow: Transform Your Business by Being Remarkable.* Portfolio, a Member of Penguin Group (USA), Inc., 2003.

Goldratt, Eliyahu, and Jeff Cox, *The Goal.* Great Barrington, MA: North River Press, 1992.

Hall, Doug and David Wecker, *The Maverick Mindset: Finding the Courage to Journey from Fear to Freedom.* Simon and Schuster, 1997.

Hamel, Gary, *Leading the Revolution.* New York: Penguin Group, 2002. Rev. ed.

Handy, Charles, *Waiting for the Mountain to Move: Reflecting on Work and Life.* San Francisco: Jossey-Bass Publishers, 1999.

Harnish, Verne, *Mastering the Rockefeller Habits: What You Must Do to Increase the Value of Your Fast Growth Firm.* SelectBooks, Inc., 2002.

Lencioni, Patrick, *The Five Temptations of a CEO.* Jossey-Bass Publishers, 1998.

Ries, Al, *Focus: The Future of Your Company Depends on It.* Harper Business, 1996.

Robbins, Anthony, *Awaken the Giant Within.* Free Press, 1992.

Senge, Peter, *The Fifth Discipline: The Art and Practice of the Learning Organization.* New York: Doubleday Currency, 1994.

Tracy, Brian, *Change Your Thinking, Change Your Life.* John Wylie and Sons, Inc., 2003.

Tracy, Brian, *Focal Point: A Proven System to Simplify Your Life, Double Your Productivity, and Achieve All Your Goals.* New York: AMACOM-American Management Association, 2001.

Tracy, Brian, *Goals! How to Get Everything You Want Faster Than You Ever Thought Possible.* San Francisco: Berrett-Koehler, 2003.

Managing Lifeblood: Time, Money and People

Adler, Lou, *Hire with Your Head.* Hoboken, NJ: John Wiley & Sons, 1998.

Kiyosaki, Robert T. with Sharon L. Lechter., CPA, *Rich Dad's Cashflow Quadrant.* Warner Business Books, 1998.

Kiyosaki, Robert T. with Sharon L. Lechter, CPA, *Rich Dad's Guide to Investing: What the Rich Invest In that the Poor and the Middle Class Do Not!* Warner Business Books, 2000.

Kiyosaki, Robert T. with Sharon L. Lechter, CPA, *Rich Kid, Smart Kid: Give Your Child a Financial Headstart.* Warner Business Books, 2001.

Kiyosaki, Robert T. with Sharon L. Lechter, CPA, *Rich Dad's Prophesy: Why the Biggest Stock Market Crash in History is Still Coming...and How You Can Prepare Yourself and Profit from It!* Warner Business Books, 2002.

Lencioni, Patrick, *The Five Dysfunctions of a Team.* Jossey-Bass Publishers, 2002.

Masterson, Michael, *Automatic Wealth, The Six Steps to Financial Independence.* 2005.

Pilzer, Paul Zane, *Unlimited Wealth: The Theory and Practice of Economic Alchemy.* Crown, 1991.

Stanley, Thomas J., Ph.D., *The Millionaire Mind.* Andrews McMeel Publishing, 2000.

Tracy, Brian, *Getting Rich Your Own Way: Achieve All Your Financial Goals Faster than You Ever Thought Possible.* John Wiley and Sons, Inc., 2004.

Strategies for Building Great Enterprise

Anderson, Dave, *Up Your Business! Seven Steps to Fix, Build, or Stretch Your Organization.* John Wiley and Sons, Inc., 2003.

Bhide, A., *The Origin and Evolution of New Businesses.* New York: Oxford University Press, 2000.

Brandt, Steven C., *Entrepreneuring: The Ten Commandments for Building a Growth Company.* Massachusetts: Addison-Wesley Publishing Company, 1983.

Brandt, Steven C., *Focus Your Business: Strategic Planning in Emerging Companies.* Friday Harbor, WA: Archipelago Publishing, 1997.

Cohn, Theodore and Roy A. Lindberg, *Survival and Growth (Management Strategies for the Small Firm.* New York: AMACOM, a Division of American Management Associations, 1978.

Drucker, Peter, *Managing for Results: Economic Tasks and Risk-Taking Decision.* New York: HarperBusiness, 1993.

Drucker, Peter, *Innovation and Entrepreneurship.* New York: HarperBusiness, 1999.

Gerber, Michael E., *The E Myth Revisited: Why Most Businesses Don't Work and What to Do About It.* Harper Business, 1995.

Gerber, Michael E., *E Myth Mastery: The Seven Essential Disciplines for Building a World Class Company.* Harper Business, 2005.

Kaplan, Robert S., and David P. Norton, *The Balanced Scorecard: Translating Strategy Into Action.* Boston: Harvard Business School Press, 1996.

Lonier, Terri, *Smart Strategies for Growing Your Business.* John Wylie and Sons, Inc., 1999.

Treacy, Michael and Fred Wiersma, *The Discipline of Market Leaders: Choose Your Customers, Narrow Your Focus, Dominate Your Market.* Reading, MA: Addison-Wesley, 1997.

Leadership Wisdom

Time with God: The New Testament for Busy People. Word Publishing Inc. 1991.

Bennis, Warren, *On Becoming a Leader.* New York: Perseus Publishing, 1994.

Catlin, Katherine and Jana Matthews, *Leading at the Speed of Growth: Journey from Entrepreneur to CEO.* Hungry Minds, Inc., 2001, Kauffman Center for Entrepenurial Leadership, Marion Ewing Kauffman Foundation.

Drucker, Peter, *The Effective Executive.* Harper and Row, 1966, 1967.

Maxwell, John C., *Developing the Leaders Around You.* Thomas Nelson Publishers, 1995.

Maxwell, John C., *The 21 Irrefutable Laws of Leadership.* Nashville: Thomas Nelson, 1998.

Maxwell, John C., *Thinking for a Change.* Warner Books, 2003.

Phillips, Donald T., *Lincoln on Leadership.* New York: Warner, 1992.

Endnotes

1   The Small Business Association, Office of Advocacy, www.sba.gov/advo
2   Ibid.
3   *Getting Rich Your Own Way*, Brian Tracy
4   Small Business Administration, Office of Advocacy
5   "Small Business: Preventing Failure—Promoting Success," Lewis A. Paul Jr., Wichita State University Small Business Development Center
6   *The Mind Map Book*, Tony Buzan

i   U.S. Small Business Administration Office of Advocacy (www.sba.gov/advo)
ii   The Small Business Administration's Office of Advocacy, www.sba.gov/advo
iii Getting Rich Your Own Way: Achieve All Your Financial Goals Faster Than You Ever Thought Possible, Brian Tracy
iv   U.S. Small Business Administration's Office of Advocacy
v   Ibid
vi   Ibid
vii U.S. Department of Labor
viii Ibid
ix   Ibid
x   Ibid
xi   U.S. Small Business Administration
xii From the publication "The Four Foundations of Great Enterprise and True Wealth" , 2000, by Sam Frowine

Also available By Sam Frowine

BLUEPRINT
FOR BUILDING
GREAT ENTERPRISE

www.SamFrowine.com

Printed in the United States
80185LV00004B/193-294